THE SECRETARY'S VISION FOR THE FUTURE— CHALLENGES AND PRIORITIES

HEARING

BEFORE THE

COMMITTEE ON HOMELAND SECURITY HOUSE OF REPRESENTATIVES

ONE HUNDRED THIRTEENTH CONGRESS

SECOND SESSION

FEBRUARY 26, 2014

Serial No. 113–53

Printed for the use of the Committee on Homeland Security

Available via the World Wide Web: http://www.gpo.gov/fdsys/

U.S. GOVERNMENT PRINTING OFFICE

88–170 PDF WASHINGTON : 2014

For sale by the Superintendent of Documents, U.S. Government Printing Office
Internet: bookstore.gpo.gov Phone: toll free (866) 512–1800; DC area (202) 512–1800
Fax: (202) 512–2250 Mail: Stop SSOP, Washington, DC 20402–0001

COMMITTEE ON HOMELAND SECURITY

MICHAEL T. MCCAUL, Texas, *Chairman*

LAMAR SMITH, Texas
PETER T. KING, New York
MIKE ROGERS, Alabama
PAUL C. BROUN, Georgia
CANDICE S. MILLER, Michigan, *Vice Chair*
PATRICK MEEHAN, Pennsylvania
JEFF DUNCAN, South Carolina
TOM MARINO, Pennsylvania
JASON CHAFFETZ, Utah
STEVEN M. PALAZZO, Mississippi
LOU BARLETTA, Pennsylvania
RICHARD HUDSON, North Carolina
STEVE DAINES, Montana
SUSAN W. BROOKS, Indiana
SCOTT PERRY, Pennsylvania
MARK SANFORD, South Carolina
VACANCY

BENNIE G. THOMPSON, Mississippi
LORETTA SANCHEZ, California
SHEILA JACKSON LEE, Texas
YVETTE D. CLARKE, New York
BRIAN HIGGINS, New York
CEDRIC L. RICHMOND, Louisiana
WILLIAM R. KEATING, Massachusetts
RON BARBER, Arizona
DONDALD M. PAYNE, JR., New Jersey
BETO O'ROURKE, Texas
TULSI GABBARD, Hawaii
FILEMON VELA, Texas
STEVEN A. HORSFORD, Nevada
ERIC SWALWELL, California

VACANCY, *Staff Director*
MICHAEL GEFFROY, *Deputy Staff Director / Chief Counsel*
MICHAEL S. TWINCHEK, *Chief Clerk*
I. LANIER AVANT, *Minority Staff Director*

CONTENTS

THE SECRETARY'S VISION FOR THE FUTURE—CHALLENGES AND PRIORITIES

Wednesday, February 26, 2014

U.S. House of Representatives,
Committee on Homeland Security,
Washington, DC.

The committee met, pursuant to call, at 10:05 a.m., in Room 311, Cannon House Office Building, Hon. Michael T. McCaul [Chairman of the committee] presiding.

Present: Representatives McCaul, Smith, King, Broun, Miller, Meehan, Duncan, Chaffetz, Palazzo, Barletta, Hudson, Brooks, Perry, Sanford, Thompson, Sanchez, Jackson Lee, Clarke, Higgins, Richmond, Keating, Barber, Payne, O'Rourke, Gabbard, Vela, Horsford, and Swalwell.

Chairman McCAUL. The Committee on Homeland Security will come to order. Committee is meeting today to hear testimony from Secretary Jeh Johnson on his vision and priorities for the Department of Homeland Security.

The committee is under several time constraints this morning, including limited availability of the Secretary, and scheduling commitments Members may have. For this reason, the Chairman will strictly enforce the 5-minute rule for questioning witnesses.

Should Members have additional questions for the witness, they will be able to ask—they can't ask during their 5 minutes, they can submit questions for the record pursuant to Committee Rules 7(e).

The Chairman appreciates Members' cooperation of moving the hearing along in an efficient manner. The Secretary will be testifying before this committee again in March with the release of the fiscal year 2015 budget. I now recognize myself for an opening statement.

Today is the 21st anniversary of the first World Trade Center Bombing, which marked the beginning of the War on Terrorism. Eight years later, the attacks on 9/11 changed our country, and re-formed our Government with the creation of the Department of Homeland Security. So it is fitting that today the new Secretary of the Department, Mr. Jeh Johnson, is here to discuss his vision for DHS.

Sir, your new position is among the most important in the Federal Government. You are at the helm of the Department, charged with securing this Nation in the midst of evolving terrorist threats, shrinking budgets, and persistent management challenges.

I appreciate sincerely, sir, your outreach to me over the past few months to discuss our shared concerns about issues of National se-

(1)

curity. I am committed to solving these challenges and look forward to working constructively with you in the future.

I just returned from New York City, where I met with the new police commissioner, Bill Bratton, and other officials, to discuss current threats. Al-Qaeda affiliates continue to target the United States.

Iran's terrorist proxies are present throughout the Western Hemisphere. A growing number of ungoverned locations across the Middle East and Northern Africa provide safe havens for Jihadist networks.

With the growing concern over lone-wolf attacks, we have to adapt to the reality that threats are not diminishing, they are evolving. DHS has a major role in identifying and mitigating terrorist threats to the homeland, whether from plots directed by jihadists, networks abroad, or from individually-inspired radicals within our borders.

The events in Syria are now threatening to become issues for us at home. I know, sir, you said in your speech at the Wilson Center, that Syria has become a matter of homeland security. I agree, and I want to hear what the Department is doing to counter this threat to the homeland.

In addition, the capture over this last weekend of the top drug lord, El Chapo Guzman, is a huge win for the United States and for Mexico. He is responsible for thousands of deaths, and his reach went far beyond Mexico.

He is public enemy No. 1 in Chicago and carries indictments in California, New York, and my home State of Texas. His arrest is significant, both symbolically and operationally. I applaud the ICE agents for their participation, along with the DEA, U.S. marshals, and Mexican authorities, for this capture. I want him to face justice in the United States, and make sure he is never out on the streets again.

As in the Guzman case, spill-over violence from drug traffic goes well beyond border towns in the United States. Pourous borders are a vulnerability to homeland security, and our border security has been woefully haphazard since 9/11.

Last year, this committee unanimously passed the Border Security Results Act, which requires the Department to create a National, strategic plan on the border, complete with metrics to check our progress. I am hopeful, with your DOD experience, sir, that you will be able to best organize your staff with both strategists and planners needed to address border security at the National strategic level. I am also hopeful the Department will work with this committee on improving our cyber defenses, which I know you have vast experience in.

The Department of Homeland Security has a critical role to play in the National Cybersecurity and Critical Infrastructure Protection Act of 2013, which we unanimously passed out of our committee earlier this month, takes an important step by codifying the Department's cybersecurity mission.

The committee would like to see a greater emphasis on building an experienced and streamlined cyber workforce, and increasing the security and resiliency of our Federal networks. All these missions will only be successful if the Department is managed efficiently.

Next week marks 11 years since the creation of DHS. No one should minimize the job of combining 22 different agencies, systems, and cultures into one. There have been many unforeseen challenges, but strong management means strong leadership.

I appreciate your sincere focus on filling the vacancies at DHS in a very short period of time since you have become appointed and confirmed. With the DHS senior leadership vacancy rate at 38 percent, I hope you will encourage the White House Presidential personnel to approve your recommendations quickly.

DHS needs competent leaders. You understand how to inspire and motivate staff, but also, how to make the tough decisions. More than 200,000 men and women whose job it is to keep Americans safe are now under your leadership.

These employees strongly believe in their mission. You briefed me on security measures also prior to the Super Bowl. I believe that the local, Federal, and private-sector collaboration that took place there is really a model for how our National security apparatus should work here at home.

I understand there is much to be proud of at the Department. I also know there is much progress to be made. I will look forward to hearing your vision and perspectives today, and for the coming years.

[The statement of Chairman McCaul follows:]

STATEMENT OF CHAIRMAN MICHAEL T. MCCAUL

FEBRUARY 26, 2014

Today is the 21st anniversary of the first World Trade Center bombing which marked the beginning of the war on terrorism. Eight years later the attacks on 9/11 changed our country and reformed our Government with the creation of the Department of Homeland Security (DHS). So it's fitting that today the new Secretary of the Department, Mr. Jeh Johnson is here to discuss his vision for DHS.

Your new position is among the most important in the Federal Government. You are at the helm of a Department charged with securing this Nation in the midst of evolving terrorist threats, shrinking budgets, and persistent management challenges.

I appreciate your outreach to me over the past few months to discuss our shared concerns about issues of National security. I am committed to solving these challenges and look forward to working constructively with you.

I just returned from New York City where I met with the new Police Commissioner Bratton and other officials to discuss current threats. Al-Qaeda affiliates continue to target the United States. Iran's terrorist proxies are present throughout the Western Hemisphere.

And a growing number of ungoverned locations across the Middle East and North Africa provide safe havens for jihadist networks. With the growing concern over lone-wolf attacks, we have to adapt to the reality that threats are not diminishing; they are evolving. DHS has a major role in identifying and mitigating terrorist threats to the U.S. homeland—whether from plots directed by jihadist networks abroad or from individually-inspired radicals within our borders.

The events in Syria are now threatening to become issues for us at home. You said in your speech at the Wilson Center, "Syria has become a matter of homeland security." I agree, and I want to hear what the Department is doing to counter this threat to the homeland.

The capture over the weekend of the drug lord, "El Chapo" Guzman is a huge win for the United States and Mexico. He is responsible for thousands of deaths and his reach went far beyond Mexico.

He is public enemy No. 1 in Chicago and carries indictments in California, New York, and my home State of Texas. His arrest is significant both symbolically and operationally and I applaud Immigration and Customs Enforcement (ICE) for their participation along with the Drug Enforcement Administration (DEA), U.S. Marshals, and Mexican authorities for this capture. I want him to face justice in the United States and make sure he is never out on the streets again.

As in the Guzman case, spillover violence from drug traffic goes well beyond border towns in the United States. Porous borders are a vulnerability to homeland security and our border security has been woefully haphazard since 9/11.

Last year this committee unanimously passed the Border Security Results Act, which requires the Department to create a National strategic plan on the border complete with metrics to check our progress.

I am hopeful with your Department of Defense (DOD) experience you will be able to best organize your staff with both strategists and planners needed to address border security at the National strategic level.

I am also hopeful the Department will work with this committee on improving our cyber defenses. The Department of Homeland Security has a critical role to play, and the *National Cybersecurity and Critical Infrastructure Protection Act of 2013,* which unanimously passed out of our committee earlier this month takes an important step by codifying the Department's cybersecurity mission. The committee would like to see a greater emphasis on building an experienced and streamlined cyber workforce and increasing the security and resiliency of Federal networks.

All of these missions will only be successful if the Department is managed efficiently. Next week marks 11 years since DHS's creation, and no one should minimize the job of combining 22 different agencies, systems, and cultures into one. There have been many unforeseen challenges but strong management means strong leadership.

I appreciate your sincere focus on filling vacancies at DHS. With the DHS senior leadership vacancy rate at 38%, I hope you will encourage White House Presidential Personnel to approve your recommendations quickly. DHS needs competent leaders who understand how to inspire and motivate staff but also make the tough decisions.

More than 200,000 men and women whose job it is to keep Americans safe are under your leadership now. These employees strongly believe in their mission. You briefed me on security measures prior to the Super Bowl and I believe the local, Federal, and private-sector collaboration that took place there is a model for how our National security apparatus should work. I understand there is much to be proud of at the Department and also know there is much progress to be made. I look forward to hearing your vision and perspectives today and for the coming years.

Chairman MCCAUL. With that, the Chairman now recognizes the Ranking Member, the gentleman from Mississippi, Mr. Thompson, for any statement he may have.

Mr. THOMPSON. Thank you, Mr. Chairman. Welcome, Mr. Secretary. I am pleased that our committee is the first in Congress to hear your vision for DHS.

I understand that the day after being sworn in as the fourth Secretary of the Department of Homeland Security, you went to New York City to the National September 11 Memorial. That quiet act reflects an appreciation of the magnitude of the job.

First and foremost, DHS was established to help make sure that America never experiences a day like that again. Specifically, DHS was established to improve terrorism prevention in safeguarding aviation and other critical infrastructure from physical and cyber threats, to achieve interoperability so that our first responders can communicate during an attack or in other emergencies, make our land, air, and sea borders more secure, and to bolster emergency preparedness, response, and resiliency at all levels.

In the 10-plus years since the Department was established, some progress has been made. But as the Comptroller General and many Members of this committee can tell you, more needs to be done for DHS to become the agency that Congress envisioned and the American people deserve.

The 233,000 men and women who serve in the Department and the 314 million Americans that it protects are looking for you to be the leader that takes DHS to the next level. Your last Federal position was at the Department of Defense. I know you have not been at DHS long, but I am sure you have noticed that the level of command and control to which you may have become accustomed to is not really there at DHS.

Last week, you experienced the potentially damaging results of this structural defect. The fact that an acquisition solicitation with significant privacy implications was published without approval by DHS, or the awareness of ICE leadership, is very troubling.

Your immediate predecessor promoted the concept of One DHS, once structural changes persist that dates back to when 22 independent offices and agencies were essentially thrown together under one roof.

As you have undoubtedly learned by now, DHS components essentially function as independent entities. All too often, components see directives from headquarters as advisory. This has to stop.

For One DHS to truly have meaning, components must adhere to Department-wide policies and mandates, and I appreciate your position when the Chairman and I had a meeting with you that you basically committed to making that happen, as well as making sure the vacancy rate at DHS would be substantially reduced.

This committee has consistently supported on a bipartisan basis granting authority to the chief officers of the Department to ensure adherence to Federal and Department-wide policies and mandates throughout DHS. Short of redoing the Federal appropriations process, this is the surest way to provide you with needed authority to prevent costly acquisition debacles and deliver timely progress on homeland security initiatives.

Mr. Secretary, there are a number of DHS programs that warrant your immediate attention. Decisions need to be made on whether to reform or in some cases end them as these programs. I urge you to ask tough questions and keep the lines of communication open with Members of this committee who have considerable knowledge about these matters.

On the subject of communication, I want to acknowledge my appreciation for the outreach to me and other Members of this committee that you have shown. We look forward to working constructively with you going forward.

With that, Mr. Chairman, I yield back.

Chairman McCAUL. I thank the Ranking Member. I associate myself with your remarks in terms of the outreach you have demonstrated to this committee. It certainly does not go unnoticed.

Members are reminded that opening statements may be submitted for the record. We are pleased today to be joined by the new appointed and confirmed Secretary. Congratulations to you.

Jeh Johnson, Secretary Johnson, was sworn in on December 23, 2013, as the fourth Secretary of the Department for Homeland Security. Prior to joining DHS, Secretary Johnson served as general counsel for the Department of Defense, where he was part of the senior management team and led more than 10,000 military and civilian lawyers across the Department.

As general counsel of the Department of Defense, Secretary Johnson oversaw the development of the legal aspects of many of our Nation's counterterrorism policies, including most importantly the successful raid on bin Laden, bringing him to justice. He also spearheaded reforms to military commissions at Guantanamo Bay in 2009.

His career includes extensive service in National security, law enforcement, as an attorney in private corporate law practice. He was also the general counsel for the Department of the Air Force from 1998 to 2001. He also served—we have this in common, sir—he also served as an assistant United States attorney. I was in a different district. You were in the southern district of New York, perhaps one of the finest, from 1989 to 1991.

His entire written statement will appear in the record. The Chairman now recognizes the Secretary for 5 minutes.

STATEMENT OF HON. JEH C. JOHNSON, SECRETARY, U.S. DEPARTMENT OF HOMELAND SECURITY

Secretary JOHNSON. Thank you, Mr. Chairman. You have my written statement submitted for the record. I would just like to give some brief comments within the 5-minute allocation.

Mr. Chairman, Ranking Member Thompson, Members of the committee, thank you for the opportunity to be here. I have appreciated your kind words, encouragement, and support in the days leading up to today's hearing. I look forward to working with this committee to meet the critical mission of homeland security.

In this, my first opportunity to testify before this committee, I would like to spell out my vision for the Department that I am privileged to lead. As each of you are aware, the Department of Homeland Security was born out of the tragic events of September 11, 2001. I am a New Yorker who was present in Manhattan on 9/11. Therefore, out of the events of that day—which happens to be my birthday—my personal commitment to the mission of homeland security was also born.

As the senior lawyer for the Department of Defense for 4 years, from 2009 through 2012, I was at the center of much of this Government's counterterrorism efforts during that period. Through the efforts of both the Bush and Obama administrations, we have put al-Qaeda's core leadership on a path to strategic defeat.

My best day as a lawyer, as the Chairman mentioned, and as a public servant, was May 1, 2011, the day our Special Forces got bin Laden.

My second best day was May 5, 2011—the day I returned to Manhattan with the President to meet with the families of the victims of 9/11. Their message to the President was simple—thank you. Bin Laden's death brought them some degree of closure, but our work must continue.

Given how the terrorist threat to this country is evolving, I welcome the opportunity to continue that work as the leader of the Department of Homeland Security.

The cornerstone of the Homeland Security mission has been and should continue to be counterterrorism—that is, protecting the Nation against terrorist attacks.

Security along our borders and at ports of entry is also a matter of homeland security. At our borders and ports of entry, we must deny entry to terrorists, drug traffickers, human traffickers, transnational criminal organizations, and other threats to National security and public safety, while—and I emphasize this—continuing to facilitate legal trade and travel.

In this regard, I, too, congratulate our law enforcement and National security partners in the government of Mexico for the capture and arrest this weekend of Joaquin "El Chapo" Guzman on February 22.

DHS must continue efforts to address the growing cyber threat to the private sector and the dot-gov networks, illustrated by the real, pervasive, and on-going series of attacks on public and private infrastructure.

Many in Congress have expressed a willingness to help in cybersecurity. We appreciate those efforts. I have studied H.R. 3696, reported out of this committee on a bipartisan basis. We think this bill is a good step forward. We want to continue working with Congress on this and other legislation to improve the Government's and the Nation's overall cybersecurity posture.

We must continue to be vigilant in preparing for and responding to disasters, including floods, wild fires, winter storms, tornadoes, hurricanes, droughts, and chemical leaks, like the one into the Elk River in West Virginia that threatened the water supply of hundreds of thousands of people.

Finally, we must be mindful of the environment in which we pursue all these missions.

First, we operate in a time of severe budget constraints. As Secretary of the Department of Homeland Security, I therefore believe I am obligated to identify and eliminate inefficiencies, waste, and unnecessary duplications of resources across DHS's large and decentralized bureaucracy, while pursuing important missions such as the recapitalization of the aging Coast Guard fleet.

Second, I am mindful of the surveys that reflect that morale is low within various components of DHS. I intend to constantly remind our workforce of the critical importance of their homeland security mission, and that the Department's greatest asset in the pursuit of these missions is our people.

I will be a champion for the men and women of DHS and I will advocate on their behalf.

I look forward to working with this committee. The Chairman is correct that I am actively working to fill the vacancies in senior management positions. I do that on a daily basis. I look forward to a shared vision and a partnership with Congress on our important mission.

Thank you.

[The prepared statement of Secretary Johnson follows:]

PREPARED STATEMENT OF HONORABLE JEH C. JOHNSON

FEBRUARY 26, 2014

Mr. Chairman, Ranking Member Thompson, and Members of this committee, thank you for the opportunity to be here. I have appreciated your kind words, encouragement, and support in the days leading up to today's hearing. I look forward to working with this committee to meet the critical mission of homeland security.

In this, my first opportunity to testify before this committee, I would like to spell out my vision for the Department I am privileged to lead.

As each of you is aware, the Department of Homeland Security (DHS) was born out of the tragic events of 9/11.

I am a New Yorker who was present in Manhattan on 9/11. Therefore, out of the events of that day, which happens to be my birthday, my personal commitment to the mission of homeland security was also born.

As the senior lawyer for the Department of Defense for 4 years from 2009 through 2012, I was at the center of much of this Government's counterterrorism efforts during that period. Through the efforts of both the Bush and Obama administrations, we have put al-Qaeda's core leadership on a path to strategic defeat. My best day as a lawyer and public servant was May 1, 2011, the day our Special Forces got bin Laden. My second best day was May 5, 2011, the day I returned to Manhattan, with the President, to meet with the families of the victims of 9/11. Their message to the President was simple: "Thank you." Bin Laden's death brought them some degree of closure, but our work must continue.

Given how the terrorist threat to this country is evolving, I welcome the opportunity to continue that work as the leader of the Department of Homeland Security.

We must remain vigilant in detecting and preventing terrorist threats that may seek to penetrate the homeland from the land, sea, or air. We must continue to build relationships with State and local law enforcement, and the first responders in our communities, to address the threats we face from those who self-radicalize to violence, the so-called "lone wolf" who may be living quietly in our midst, inspired by radical, violent ideology to do harm to Americans—illustrated last year by the Boston Marathon bombing.

Addressing each of these types of threats is a matter for the Department of Homeland Security in close collaboration with other departments and agencies.

The cornerstone of the homeland security mission has been, and should continue to be, counterterrorism; that is, protecting the Nation against terrorist attacks.

Security along our borders and at ports of entry is also a matter of homeland security. At our borders and ports of entry, we must deny entry to terrorists, drug traffickers, human traffickers, transnational criminal organizations, and other threats to National security and public safety while continuing to facilitate legal travel and trade.

We must be agile in addressing threats to border security. We must dedicate resources where the threats exist, and be prepared to move when they move.

We are gratified by the support Congress has provided to improve security at our borders and ports of entry. With that support, we've made great progress. There is now more manpower, technology, and infrastructure on our borders than ever before, and our men and women in and around the border are producing results.

For example, on February 10, a task force led by U.S. Immigration and Customs Enforcement shut down a 481-foot drug smuggling tunnel between Nogales, Mexico and Nogales, Arizona, arrested three men involved in the smuggling operation, and seized 640 pounds of marijuana.

Meanwhile, our law enforcement and National security partners in the government of Mexico are making great strides in our common interest of combating drug trafficking, violence, and illicit activity along our shared border, marked by the operation to capture Joaquin "Chapo" Guzman Loera, the alleged leader of the Sinaloa Cartel, on February 22. We congratulate the government of Mexico for these efforts.

As you know, more needs to be done.

The day in January I visited the Port Isabel Detention Center near Brownsville, Texas, I saw about 1,000 detainees, 18% of whom were Mexican, and the rest representing over 30 different nationalities who migrated through Mexico in an effort to get to the United States.

Smuggling organizations are responsible for almost all those who cross the border illegally. We must attack these networks. And when individuals are detained in our custody, we must ensure our detention facilities are safe and humane.

And, as part of reforming our immigration system, we support the additional border and port security resources that common-sense immigration reform legislation would provide.

The President, many Members of Congress, the business and labor communities, and others all recognize that immigration reform is a matter of economic growth. In my view, immigration reform is also a matter of homeland security. There are an estimated 11.5 million undocumented immigrants living in this country. Most have been here for years. Many came here as children. I believe that, as a matter of homeland security, we should encourage these people to come out of the shadows of American society, pay taxes and fines, be held accountable, and be given the opportunity to get on a path to citizenship like others. Allowing individuals to come out of the shadows will also allow DHS to dedicate even more focus and attention on public safety, National security, and border security threats. I support common-sense immigration reform and the additional resources it would bring.

DHS must continue efforts to address the growing cyber threat to the private sector and the ".gov" networks, illustrated by the real, pervasive, and on-going series of attacks on public and private infrastructure.

In this effort, I believe that, for DHS, building trust and relationships with the private sector is crucial.

Through the President's Executive Order 13636 on critical infrastructure cybersecurity, and Presidential Policy Directive 21 on strengthening the security and resilience of critical infrastructure, we are continuing to strengthen our partnerships with the private sector.

On February 12, the White House made public the "Cybersecurity Framework," which is a set of best practices and voluntary guidelines for the private sector. Initial reports are the Framework has received a positive reaction from the private sector. That same day, DHS stood up for public use the Critical Infrastructure Cyber Community—or "C³"—Voluntary Program, which gives companies direct access to cybersecurity experts within DHS who have knowledge of the threats we face. There is more to do.

I believe it is crucial that, for the cybersecurity mission to succeed, we must recruit the next generation of cybersecurity talent to serve in Government. For this, I have embarked on a personal recruitment campaign. On February 14, I visited Georgia Tech and Morehouse College to encourage students there interested in cybersecurity to consider public service. I am planning other visits to colleges and universities for the same purpose.

Many in Congress have expressed a willingness to help in cybersecurity. We appreciate those efforts. I have studied H.R. 3696 reported out of this committee on a bipartisan basis. We think this bill is a good step forward. We want to continue working with Congress on this and other legislation to improve the Government and Nation's overall cybersecurity posture.

We must continue to be vigilant in preparing for and responding to disasters, including floods, wildfires, winter storms, tornadoes, hurricanes, droughts, and chemical leaks like the one into the Elk River in West Virginia that threatened the water supply of hundreds of thousands of people.

FEMA has come a long way from the days after Hurricane Katrina. We have improved disaster planning with public and private-sector partners, non-profit organizations, and the American people. We have learned how to pre-position a greater number of resources and we have helped to strengthen the Nation's ability to respond to disasters in a quick and robust fashion.

For example, on Tuesday, February 11, the President signed an emergency declaration in response to the severe winter storm that rolled through Georgia that week. By 6 p.m. on Thursday February 13, FEMA had shipped to the State 112 generators, 453,000 liters of water, over 1,000,000 meals, over 7,000 blankets, over 2,000 cots, and 2,500 tarps.

We must continue good work like this.

We must be mindful of the environment in which we pursue these missions:

First, we operate in a time of severe budget constraints. The days are over when those of us in National and homeland security can expect more and more to be added each year to our top-line budgets. As Secretary of the Department of Homeland Security, I believe I am obliged to identify and eliminate inefficiencies, waste, and unnecessary duplications of resources across DHS's large and decentralized bureaucracy, while pursuing important missions such as the recapitalization of the aging Coast Guard fleet.

I compliment TSA for its recent decision to realign the number of Federal Air Marshal offices across the country, to achieve greater efficiencies while continuing to perform this critical mission, and I am encouraging other DHS components to think in these terms.

To achieve greater efficiencies, we must manage our large and diffuse bureaucracy more effectively. I am pleased that late last year DHS received its first unqualified, or "clean," audit opinion, a significant achievement just 10 years after the largest realignment and consolidation of U.S. Government agencies and functions since the creation of the Department of Defense. At my direction, we are also working to get DHS programs off the GAO "high-risk" list.

Second, I am mindful of the surveys that reflect that morale is low within various components of DHS. I intend to constantly remind our workforce of the critical importance of their homeland security mission, and that the Department's greatest asset in the pursuit of that mission is our people.

I will be a champion for the men and women of DHS, and I will advocate on their behalf.

I did not enjoy, early in my tenure, suspending Administratively Uncontrollable Overtime pay for certain categories of DHS workers. I continue to support overtime for DHS personnel who earn it and require it, especially the men and women in the field working to keep our Nation safe, but we must work within the laws and rules pursuant to which overtime is sought and received.

We must inject a new energy into DHS, and good leadership starts with recruiting other good leaders to join the team to help run the organization. With the help of the White House and Congress, we are actively recruiting terrific people to fill the large number of senior management vacancies that have existed within DHS.

We look forward to the Senate confirmation of Suzanne Spaulding to be under secretary for National Protection and Programs Directorate; Gil Kerlikowske to be the next commissioner of Customs and Border Protection; John Roth to be the next inspector general; Leon Rodriguez to be the next director of U.S. Citizenship and Immigration Services; and Dr. Reggie Brothers to be the next under secretary for Science and Technology.

I am very pleased that on February 12 the President nominated retired Brigadier General Frank Taylor, the former ambassador-at-large for counterterrorism, to be our next under secretary for Intelligence & Analysis. We are working to recruit terrific people to fill other key positions, including the next under secretary for Management, director of Immigration and Customs Enforcement, and the Chief Financial Officer.

Finally, the Department's ability to serve the American people well requires effective oversight by Congress. I want to work with this committee to reform DHS Congressional jurisdiction, which is spread across more than 100 committees and subcommittees of Congress. More than 10 years after the Department's creation, it is time to fulfill this 9/11 Commission recommendation and streamline the current oversight structure.

For my part, I have directed my staff and our component leadership to be responsive to inquiries and letters from Members and committees of Congress. I have begun a practice of personally reading each letter addressed to me from any Member of Congress, and, along with the deputy secretary, I track the status to ensure you receive the responses promptly.

In all, I believe DHS must be agile and vigilant in continually adapting to evolving threats and hazards. We must learn from and adapt to the changing character of the threats and hazards we face: 9/11; Hurricane Katrina in 2005; the underwear bomber in 2009; the Deepwater Horizon oil spill in 2010; Hurricane Sandy in 2012; and the Boston Marathon bombing in 2013 illustrate these evolving threats and hazards. We must stay one step ahead of the next terrorist attack, the next cyber attack, and the next natural disaster.

In the pursuit of this important mission, I pledge to this committee my total dedication and all the energy I possess.

Thank you for listening and I look forward to your questions.

Chairman McCAUL. I thank the Secretary, and I believe that your priorities and mine are very similar. We look forward to working with you on achieving those.

This last weekend was an extraordinary weekend for me, having been the chief of counterterrorism, who at the U.S.-Mexico border, my jurisdiction, the drug cartels have been on my radar screen for quite some time. The arrest of the largest, most well-known drug lord of the most powerful, oldest drug cartel organization, the Sinaloa, was hugely significant.

He has smuggled tons of drugs into the United States, killed thousands of people. I want to personally take this opportunity to thank Homeland Security officials, ICE agents on the ground who made this happen, who worked closely with DEA to bring Chapo Guzman finally, after 3 decades, to justice.

I think it is important that we recognize our men and women in Homeland Security who had a role in bringing him down.

I am concerned, and I did talk to the Ambassador from Mexico yesterday, we had a very good conversation. He is very proud of the cooperation between the United States and Mexico, which was extraordinary in this case. Mexico is to be commended for their willingness to take this threat on, head-on. They took down the head of the Los Zetas cartel and now with Chapo Guzman, Sinaloa.

As you know, Mr. Secretary, El Chapo Guzman escaped captivity, a prison, in 2001. He has 12 years left to his sentence. But I am concerned about that happening again in Mexico. My understanding is that extradition papers have not been served to date.

Do you know whether this administration is intent on extraditing El Chapo Guzman to the United States to stand trial for the crimes he committed in the United States?

Secretary JOHNSON. Mr. Chairman, let me begin by echoing much of what you said. We do indeed have a terrific partnership with the government of Mexico in our shared homeland security, border security efforts. We work together constantly.

I was in Mexico with the President last week. I intend to go back in the next couple of weeks. I intend to speak with my Mexican counterpart today on various matters. So I can't emphasize enough the importance and the strength of our shared law enforcement, homeland security, National security efforts. We work well together as a team with the government of Mexico.

I, too, agree with the importance and the broad implications of this weekend's capture and arrest.

Mr. Chairman, as you know, extradition is a matter for the Department of Justice. I have read what you have read with great interest. One of the things that strikes me about where we are, it may be easier to work out the appropriate arrangement with the government of Mexico than it will be to work out an appropriate arrangement among the six U.S. attorneys who would like to prosecute this individual. That will be an interesting discussion.

But I have to respectfully refer you to the Department of Justice with regard to the discussions that I know they are having with the government of Mexico regarding extradition.

Chairman MCCAUL. Well, you are a part of this administration. I would hope that having a seat at the table, you will urge the Attorney General and the State Department, as I am doing, to seek extradition and bring him to the United States for trial. I would hope that you would agree with that assessment.

Secretary JOHNSON. I agree wholeheartedly that we in this country have an interest in seeing him brought to justice.

Chairman MCCAUL. Well, and I know that there are multiple jurisdictions here at play. I am going to do everything in my power to see that that happens.

You talked about Syria in your speech at the Wilson Center. You said that Syria is now a matter of homeland security. I couldn't agree with you more, as we see more and more jihadists pouring into Syria for the fight in the rebel forces who have been now infiltrated by al-Qaeda affiliates. It is becoming one of the largest training grounds now in the world, in my judgment, surpassing the FATA in Pakistan.

Therein lies the threat, I think, to the United States. These individuals have travel documents, with training, expertise, leaving Syria, perhaps going to Western Europe or the United States is a serious concern of mine. I would like for you to elaborate on that statement.

Secretary JOHNSON. From my experience at the Department of Defense in counterterrorism matters, I know that terrorist organizations look for places to build safe havens. They look for places in remote areas, in areas that do not have robust law enforcement, to train and from which to launch terrorist attacks and terrorist planning.

So we have to be constantly vigilant in looking out for those efforts and preventing them. I have seen that time and again over the 4 years I was at the Department of Defense. We are concerned about foreign fighters going into Syria. It is a shared concern between us and our European allies and others in the world.

The numbers are concerning. We are monitoring the situation very closely. I would say that for those of us in National security and homeland security in this government, this particular issue is at the top of the list or near the top of the list for us. We talk about it all the time. We are carefully monitoring the situation, and I would be happy to share with this committee in a non-public setting some of the more sensitive elements of what our Government is doing.

I believe at least several of you may have been briefed on that, but we are happy to share that information.

Chairman MCCAUL. We appreciate that information. Thank you, Secretary.

The Chairman now recognizes the Ranking Member.

Mr. THOMPSON. Thank you very much, Mr. Chairman.

Again, welcome, Mr. Secretary. Recently, TSA decided to open a pre-clearance operation in Abu Dhabi. Some of us have expressed concern that it might in our estimation have been a rush that could potentially create some vulnerabilities for people traveling to the United States.

I think one of the issues is that people coming from Abu Dhabi would bypass the domestic screening when boarding connecting flights in the United States. Some of those people are identified as selectees.

So if I am coming to New York, Dulles, or LAX, can you assure this committee that the process TSA has implemented would somehow allow the selectees to be more than just passed through? That once they touched down in the United States, there would be some kind of re-screening of that individual once they are here?

Secretary JOHNSON. Thank you, Congressman, for that question.

The short answer to your question is yes, that is something that is important that I intend to look at, in terms of what happens at the arrival, once somebody has gone through pre-clearance overseas.

I want to emphasize what I regard as the importance of pre-clearance at our last point-of-departure airports. Aviation security involves, in my judgment, primarily security when it concerns what happens in the air on the way to the United States. We got a rude awakening of that on December 25, 2009.

So, in my judgment, looking at the security at the various last point-of-departure airports that are out there in the world that send flights into the United States, I believe it is a homeland security imperative that we improve that security in one way or another. I think pre-clearance is a good way to do that.

Abu Dhabi is not intended to be an endpoint. It is a point along the way in a progression. We will continue to look at additional airports and I think we ought to also look at your question, as well—what happens when the traveler gets to the United States.

Mr. THOMPSON. Especially when some of the travelers have been ping'd in the system as a selectee. I am concerned about—because we have a number of those individuals who would come through that. I look forward to working with you on that.

Chairman, I would like unanimous consent that the letter to the committee received from the Airline Pilots Association expressing concern with the pre-clearance operation in Abu Dhabi be inserted in the record.

Chairman MCCAUL. Without objection, so ordered.

[The information follows:]

LETTER FROM THE AIR LINE PILOTS ASSOCIATION INTERNATIONAL

FEBRUARY 25, 2014.

The Honorable MICHAEL MCCAUL,
Chairman, Committee on Homeland Security, 176 Ford Office Building, Washington, DC 20515.

The Honorable BENNIE THOMPSON,
Ranking Member, Committee on Homeland Security, 117 Ford Office Building, Washington, DC 20515.

DEAR CHAIRMAN MCCAUL AND RANKING MEMBER THOMPSON: On behalf of the 50,000 professional airline pilots represented by the Air Line Pilots Association, International (ALPA), we would like to thank you for holding a hearing on future priorities and challenges at the U.S. Department of Homeland Security (DHS). We recognize that DHS faces monumental tasks and are pleased to partner with your committee and Secretary Johnson's team to address aviation security challenges.

ALPA continues to oppose the Customs and Border Protection (CBP) preclearance facility at Abu Dhabi International Airport. The lack of U.S. air carrier service to Abu Dhabi as well as the unusual pay-to-play precedent that is being set by CBP with regard to future preclearance facilities is extremely troubling and aggravates the immediate CBP staffing challenges at our domestic airports.

The very real threat posed by Middle Eastern air carriers to the future of the U.S. aviation industry is further exacerbated by our own country's willingness to provide these foreign carriers with a competitive financial advantage by authorizing these preclearance facilities. The direct and indirect financial and policy support these foreign air carriers receive from their respective governments already provides them with a competitive advantage. They don't need our help.

In addition to ALPA's opposition to the Abu Dhabi site, we are particularly concerned with recent reports of another preclearance facility being planned less than 100 miles away in Dubai. If these reports are true, and another preclearance facility is in fact planned for Dubai, then our initial concerns with respect to Abu Dhabi and the "domino effect" it will have on other Middle Eastern airports are fully substantiated. If anything, this situation has highlighted the need for a clear and uniform policy on how future preclearance sites are established, but more importantly, the need for Congressional oversight and approval of any such facilities.

We appreciate the committee's commitment to ensuring sound security oversight related to any expansion of preclearance facilities and hope that you will continue to explore the security questions surrounding Abu Dhabi preclearance. Further, we respectfully impress upon you that any expansion of CBP preclearance facilities that present an unlevel playing field for U.S. carriers is poor policy and will have serious ramifications for the U.S. airline industry and U.S. jobs.

Thank you for your continued interest in this matter.

Sincerely,

LEE MOAK,
President.

Mr. THOMPSON. Secretary, several years ago, Congress passed 100 percent screening mandate for maritime cargo. Your predecessor looked at it and said we didn't need to do it. Will you look at the 100 percent screening mandate that Congress passed and report back to us on where we are toward meeting that mandate?

Secretary JOHNSON. That legal mandate is something that many Members of Congress have talked to me, too—talked to me about, including in the Senate confirmation process, it was raised by a number of Members of Congress on both sides of the aisle.

As recently as last week when I was at the port of Los Angeles, I examined what our screening scanning capabilities are and the implications of putting that—trying to put that and the cost of putting that at overseas ports to comply with the legal requirement. I understand that the Secretary of Homeland Security can, for a period of time, waive that. I am looking at that.

In general, I believe that the Department ought to comply with legal mandates. So if there is some reason we can't immediately, then consistent with the law, we ought to at least have a plan for getting there.

So I am studying the issue very closely, and I did that as recently as last week.

Mr. THOMPSON. Thank you. I yield back, Mr. Chairman.

Chairman MCCAUL. The Chairman will now recognize other Members for 5 minutes for questions in the order of arrival.

The Chairman now recognizes the gentleman from Texas, Mr. Smith.

Mr. SMITH. Thank you, Mr. Chairman.

Secretary Johnson, let me switch to the subject of immigration. The administration has been making a sales pitch that they are deporting or removing record numbers of individuals compared to previous administrations.

You all count, do you not, the turn-arounds, the turn-backs at the border, as deportations?

Secretary JOHNSON. Yes, Congressman. I believe that was reflected in the removal numbers we reported recently for fiscal year 2013.

Mr. SMITH. That is correct. That is correct. That is reflected in your deportation numbers. The problem is other administrations, including the Bush administration and the Clinton administration, did not include turn-backs at the border as a part of their deportation numbers.

So to say that you are setting records when comparing oranges and oranges is simply not accurate. If you look at interior deportations, they are down 40 percent since 2009. Do you agree with that generally speaking, if we are looking at interior deportation? You may need to check that, I realize.

But I have looked at the figures, and they are down 40 percent. So for this administration to say it is breaking records in removing individuals is simply not accurate. If you have any comment on that, you are welcome to make it.

Secretary JOHNSON. Well, I would have to look at the the numbers myself. My understanding, which could be wrong, is that consistent with prior administrations, we have reported the overall numbers; but that with respect to the last report, we broke out, within that overall number, the number of those who are border arrests——

Mr. SMITH. Again, the problem with this administration is that they are including the turn-backs and the removals by the Border Patrol at the border. Previous administrations did not. So you are inflating your figures so that you can claim to be setting records, when in fact, you are not.

Actual deportations from the interior are down 40 percent. If you want to get back to me on that, you are welcome to.

Secretary JOHNSON. I will look into those numbers, sir.

Mr. SMITH. Okay. Let me go to another subject, and that is what the administration is doing with illegal immigrants who have been charged with serious crimes. As I understand it, the administration is releasing tens of thousands of these individuals back into our communities where they are of course a threat to American citizens and residents.

I was not able to get the figures from the Department of Homeland Security, but I was able to get the figures from the Congressional Research Service, though they are I think a year old. Fourteen percent of those individuals who have been charged and released were charged with DUI; 10 percent, drug violations; 7 percent, thousands of people, charged with murder, assault, rape, and kidnapping, were released back into our communities. Why?

Secretary JOHNSON. What I am committed to do is removing those who represent National security, public safety, and border security threats. I believe that that requires a constant reevaluation of our process, what we are doing, who we are removing. I am committed to continuing to do that.

Mr. SMITH. Shouldn't individuals in our country illegally, who have been charged with these kinds of crimes, shouldn't they be a priority to remove? Why would we release them back in our streets, and communities, and neighborhoods?

Secretary JOHNSON. Those who represent public safety threats who are in this country illegally fit within our removal priorities.

Mr. SMITH. Do you not think they represent a public threat, these individuals who have been charged with those crimes?

Secretary JOHNSON. Well, as I said, I think we should continually reevaluate what we are doing to make sure that what we are doing fit within those priorities.

Mr. SMITH. In your reevaluation, I hope you will give greater priority to removing those individuals who are clearly a threat to the lives and safety of American citizens, and who have been charged with these crimes, tens of thousands of people. You are actually releasing more people into our neighborhoods than you are removing of the individuals who have been charged with crimes. I just don't know what the justification or rationale, for that is.

Last question goes to border security: As you probably know, in 2011, the Government Accountability Office came up with the determination that about 44 percent of the border was under some level of control, but that only 6.5 percent of the border was under actual control—6.5 percent.

The administration didn't like that result, so they said, "We are not going to use the GAO's metrics anymore. We are going to come up with something else."

To this day, they have not. So we have no way of knowing, as we sit here right now, how secure or insecure the border is, other than 6.5 percent a few years ago was actually under actual control. When is the DHS going to update its border security statistics?

Secretary JOHNSON. I agree with the goal of establishing metrics for what constitutes border security. I agree with that goal. We are working toward that goal right now, and we are working towards something we can share with Congress.

When I was at the Southwest Border, and I talked to the border-security experts about border security, they emphasized to me an approach that is agile, with an emphasis on surveillance, with an emphasis on mobility, so that we can follow the threats as they exist, as we can follow the trends in illegal migration as they arise. I think that is a good approach. I think that with the resources Congress has given us, we have done better. But there is always more work to do.

Chairman McCAUL. Chairman now recognizes the gentlelady from California, Ms. Sanchez.

Ms. SANCHEZ. Thank you, Mr. Chairman. Secretary, it is great to have you. Of course, seen you before the House Armed Services Committee before, and really excited to have you over at the Department. Have a lot of questions for you, so I am going to sort of go through them, and maybe if you have a pencil there, what have you.

First of all, I want to put into the record, with unanimous consent, Mr. Chairman, a letter from the Coalition for Humane Immigrant Rights of Los Angeles to be into the record, please.

Chairman McCAUL. Without objection, so ordered.

[The information follows:]

LETTER FROM THE COALITION FOR HUMANE IMMIGRANT RIGHTS OF LOS ANGELES

FEBRUARY 25, 2014.

The Honorable Michael McCaul,
Chairman, Committee on Homeland Security, 176 Ford Office Building, Washington, DC 20515.

The Honorable BENNIE THOMPSON,
Ranking Member, Committee on Homeland Security, 117 Ford Office Building, Washington, DC 20515.

DEAR CHAIRMAN McCAUL AND RANKING MEMBER THOMPSON: The Coalition for Humane Immigrant Rights of Los Angeles (CHIRLA) is a regional organization whose mission is to advance the human and civil rights of immigrants and refugees in Los Angeles. CHIRLA advocates on behalf of this community through policy & advocacy, organizing, education and community building. On behalf of CHIRLA, I am writing to express our views and issue recommendations for the hearing on immigration border enforcement to be held on 26 February 2014, "The Secretary's Vision for the Future—Challenges and Priorities."

As an organization with a strong commitment to its members to do its utmost to advance the cause of immigration reform, we wish to reiterate our support for this committee's measured bipartisan approach to border security as outlined in the Chairman's bill, H.R. 1417. Unfortunately, similarly sensible action has to date neither been taken by the House Judiciary Committee nor has H.R. 1417 or any other immigration bill been brought to the floor for debate or a single vote. While we will continue to push for fair, inclusive reform that will recognize the contributions hard work of millions of immigrants, CHIRLA and its allies feel strongly that the Department of Homeland Security can and should act to provide relief for our communities in the mean time. To our mind, it is both counterproductive and fundamentally un-American to deport the very same people who ultimately would benefit from the passage of such reform, simply due to the fact that they were arbitrarily entangled in the tentacles of immigration enforcement.

Accordingly, we propose the following as topics of concern to the immigrant community and should therefore be at the forefront of the Secretary and the administration's work to help guide the country towards a solution to our broken immigration system:

- *Deferred Action for Childhood Arrivals (DACA).*—Department of Homeland Security (DHS) should not only focus on the renewal process, but also on updating the language and requirements to ensure that a broader portion of the eligible population is covered;
- Keep families, including but not limited to those with DACA recipients, together by expanding upon administrative relief options;
- In concert with the Executive Office of Immigration Review at the Department of Justice, DHS should implement a broader use of prosecutorial discretion as outlined in the Morton memos dated 17 June 2011 and 3 March 2011;[1]
- Designate the nationals of the Philippines as eligible for Temporary Protected Status (TPS) due to the on-going crisis following Typhoon Haiyan;
- Recommend a far greater appropriation of DHS monies towards the integration of New Americans rather than further strengthening the enforcement apparatus that instead removes aspiring Americans from this country;
- Require that all ICE detainers (1–247), whether issued by a Federal agent or a 287(g) cross-deputized local law enforcement officer, be co-signed by a supervisory official at a DHS headquarters;
- Exercise greater vigilance regarding racial profiling. Follow through on the DHS Officer for Civil Rights and Civil Liberties (OCRCL) commitments to statistically evaluate unconstitutional and disparate impact of immigration enforcement programs such as "Secure Communities".

We look forward to seeing the above can be implemented by the Department, and would be happy to discuss this in greater detail with Members of the committee and their staff.

Sincerely,

JOSEPH VILLELA,
Director of Policy & Advocacy.

Ms. SANCHEZ. Second, Mr. Secretary, here are my questions. The first is a plea, if you will, I know that you understand, or are trying to understand what is going on in Venezuela right now. There is not as much of an emphasis of what is going on in Venezuela vis-á-vis the TV reporting, et cetera, as the Ukraine, for example.

But the fact of the matter is it is getting incredibly dangerous, and a lot of people are suffering. So my first would be just to remind your USCIS agents who are dealing with some of these visas that people are on from Venezuela, that in a time of such instability and almost a civil war going on there, that they have a lot of discretion in being able to extend some of that time, or helping those people stay here until it gets better in the situation over there in Venezuela. I think that is incredibly important for you to reiterate, please, with the people that you oversee.

Second, we have a particular situation on the California-Mexico border. Been working a long time. As you know, Mexico has been—this is between Mexicali and Calexico. I know the area well, because my mother grew up in the Mexicali area.

So the waits are 2 or 3 hours, sometimes, in the pedestrian line, to walk across. There is a lot of cross-traffic that happens. People live in one place, they work in the other, vice versa.

Mexicali gets up to about 125 degrees in the summer. Summer is coming up. There are no shade areas for these people as they stand in line. I know that the local chamber there is coming up with about half the money.

It would take about a million dollars to kind of restructure the pedestrian piece of processing, where they could get a much faster

---

[1] 2/3/11 "Civil Immigration Enforcement: Priorities for the Apprehension, Detention, and Removal of Aliens:"; 6/17/11 "Prosecutorial Discretion: Certain Victims, Witnesses, and Plaintiffs" and "Exercising Prosecutorial Discretion Consistent with the Civil Immigration Enforcement Priorities of the Agency for the Apprehension, Detention, and Removal of Aliens".

flow-through, you know, without any increase in risk of who is coming across.

I would urge you, please, to take a look, and to help us get that done before the summer months come, because it really affects a lot of people. It is—you know, a million bucks is not a lot when we are talking about the Federal Government. It would really, really help there.

TWIC cards, just want to get some indication from you. With the readers not working, what do you see as the future of what is going on with the whole TWIC card situation?

The next one, of course, I have been a big advocate of the U.S. exit biometrics to exit, understanding the visas that we allow people to come in on, and then they overstay. Quite frankly, the former Secretary sat in front of us the first time she was there, and said she just wasn't going to do it.

We have passed it in law twice. This committee has passed it two or three times. Mrs. Miller and I have a bill to try to get that done. So I would be very interested in that.

Last, you have a lot of experience from the Defense Department. What can you bring? How can you help us to get things more streamlined, more categorized, and better off in this Department? Again, thank you for your service.

Secretary JOHNSON. Item No. 1, I would be happy to look at the letter that was put into the record. I would like to mention, ma'am, that I was in Los Angeles Friday, and met with a coalition of those interested in immigration enforcement and reform. We had a good meeting at the City Hall with the mayor.

No. 2, thank you for your reference to Venezuela. It is obviously a situation we are looking at closely. But I appreciate the context in which you mention it.

No. 3, on the issue of wait times, that is something I will look at, particularly in the port of entry you mentioned. I do know that wait times, whether it is at a land port or an airport, can spike up or down, depending on circumstances. But I am happy to look at that as well.

With regard to TWIC cards, I think the overall goal of the card, the overall Homeland Security goal is a good one, and a valid one. I think it is a program that we need to continue to develop and pursue.

In the development of such a program like that, there are always a few things that could be done more efficiently. I know that a number of truckers, for example, would like to see it be done, you know, sort of one-stop shopping, versus having to visit two or three times. I understand that, and I think we will get there.

Biometric exit is, in my judgment, the gold standard. It is a place that we eventually ought to get to. I have asked about it. We have biometric entry.

I would like to ultimately see us get to biometric exit. There are some practical and cost considerations to doing that. But it is the gold standard. I agree with that.

Ms. SANCHEZ. Thank you, Mr. Secretary. I look forward to hopefully—to having an individual meeting, maybe going more in-depth on some of these issues, because I think they are incredibly important.

Secretary JOHNSON. It is nice to see you again as well.

Ms. SANCHEZ. Thank you.

Chairman MCCAUL. Chairman now recognizes Chairman Emeritus, Mr. King.

Mr. KING. Thank you, Mr. Chairman. Let me also, at the outset, thank you for the visit you made to New York on Monday. From talking to the commissioner afterwards, it was a very, very fruitful meeting. I thank you for the interest you have shown.

Secretary Johnson, I want to welcome you to the committee. Thank you for the interest and the outreach you have done since your nomination, and certainly since your approval by the Senate.

It was mentioned that 21 years ago today was the first attack on the World Trade Center. Actually, a neighbor of mine, Monica Rodriguez Schmitz, was killed that day. I think a mistake all of us made, was none of us realized the full implications of that.

As you said, you were in New York on 9/11 itself. We did respond very strongly to that. As you said, under both administrations, we have gone a long way toward decimating the leadership of al-Qaeda, of core al-Qaeda.

I guess a concern I have is that all of us, perhaps, you know, to make sure that we don't make the mistake we made after 1993 and not realize the full extent of the threat. Because, as you mentioned, regarding Syria, and the Chairman has mentioned also, al-Qaeda has now metastasized and morphed. So core al-Qaeda is no longer probably the main threat we face.

In your speech, you mentioned Syria. But also, there is Egypt, Iraq, Libya, Yemen, Algeria, Mali, Somalia, all of which have organizations with either—direct relations to al-Qaeda, or they share the al-Qaeda philosophy.

What is the Department of Homeland Security doing to adapt to the threats that could be coming from those countries, specifically like with Syria, where we would have people who are foreign fighters, who could have come from visa-waiver countries, or they could be U.S. citizens, or the other countries that were mentioned. How is DHS adapting to this new type of terror we are facing?

Secretary JOHNSON. Thank you for that question, Congressman. I think, from my Homeland Security perspective, which includes TSA, CBP, CIS, ICE, Coast Guard, information sharing with our partners through which individuals of suspicion may travel, we need greater information sharing.

We need greater attention to the borders, not just the U.S. borders. It is something we are working on. It is something that I worked on with our allies, as recently as 2 weeks ago when I met with our European counterparts, Syria was the issue at the top of the list.

I think greater attention to aviation security and port security. That is why I mentioned that in my judgment, pre-clearance is very, very important from a Homeland Security perspective. I think we need to build on that.

I think we need to continue to build on intelligence information sharing across JTTFs, fusion centers, with the intelligence community and Homeland Security. I think information sharing is key. I am also concerned about those who self-radicalize. I think you share that concern about the so-called lone wolf. I think that the

Boston Marathon bombing may be a sign of the future. In many respects, those threats are harder to detect.

So working with State and local governments, first responders, police commissioners, fire departments, funding, training, preparedness—and we saw, I think, a decent example of how that training and preparedness can work in places like Boston if another tragedy happens.

So I think we have got to be vigilant. I think the terrorist threat is becoming more diffuse. In many respects, it is harder to detect. Beginning in around 2009, we saw a rise of affiliates. But I think it is becoming even more diffuse.

Mr. KING. Secretary, whenever the Secretary of Homeland Security comes in, we were always critical of the fact the Department is not run efficiently enough. Yet, looking at ourselves, we have, I think, 110 Congressional committees, and subcommittees, which have just totally spread jurisdiction all over the place when it comes to homeland security.

In this, I would say, both parties have failed to really address this. I would just ask, as we have asked other secretaries, to try to use whatever influence you might have with the Congress, just to make it clear, the terrible drain on your time that it involves, and also, the fact that you can't respond to that many masters. I mean, basically, Defense Department has asked.

You, now in your capacity, have 110 committees and subcommittees. So whatever you could do just to lend your voice to that would be appreciated.

Secretary JOHNSON. I hesitate to tell you folks how to do your job. That is your prerogative. But I do agree that when I have 108 committees and subcommittees of Congress performing an oversight function, it takes a lot of time to—and I enjoy coming up here. But it takes a lot of time to deal with all of the oversight, which detracts from the core mission that I think you want me to pay attention to.

Mr. KING. Mr. Chairman, I just have 10 seconds on this. There is a matter which I will talk to you privately about. There is an individual I am aware of, who I believe has been watch-listed for a number of years. I have met with Homeland Security, with TSC, FBI, to try to resolve this issue.

Unfortunate to say, since I have been asking questions, his treatment seems to be worse; yesterday, a terrible incident at an airport. I will discuss it with you privately. This is not primarily your responsibility, but again, TSA does have some bearing here.

So I just wanted to discuss it with you privately. I don't want to cause any extra problem for this person by mentioning his name publicly. But I will get back to you on that.

Secretary JOHNSON. Glad to take that for the record.

Mr. KING. Thank you.

Chairman McCAUL. Thank the gentleman. Let me also say, I agree with the jurisdictional problems. I think it detracts from your mission. It is something I would like to fix. We have a hearing scheduled on this issue.

The Aspen Institute came out with a very good video called "Homeland Confusion." So with that, I recognize the gentlelady from Texas, Ms. Sheila Jackson Lee.

Ms. JACKSON LEE. Thank you very much, Mr. Chairman, for this hearing. Secretary, again, thank you for your commitment to service.

Might I just echo two of my preceding colleagues. It would be great if we, ourselves, self-regulated ourselves with respect to the streamline of committees that address the question of homeland security. So I hope that we will have the opportunity to do so. We hope the administration would be supportive, as they can be, with the three branches of Government.

Let me very quickly add my appreciation for the apprehension of Guzman, and all that that represents, particularly the heroic efforts of ICE and the U.S. Marshals, DEA, Mexican authorities. It is a very important statement.

I join my colleague for indicating that I am respectful of Mexican sovereignty. But I think we are neighbors and collaborators, and I believe it would be very important that we have the ability for Mr. Guzman to be transferred here to the United States under the necessary procedures.

I also want to thank you, as the Secretary of Homeland Security, for your forceful comments during Sochi regarding the security of our athletes, and all the efforts that were made by Americans that complemented the work that was done in Europe and in Russia. We are very thankful for the safe return of our athletes.

I want to quickly ask some questions. I am going to say them, then hopefully, you will be able to answer them. I want to go specifically to the question of detention.

I think we have had some discussions, and the whole idea of the fact that we are detaining through ICE. We have gone from 167,000 to 478,000. There has not been much use of the alternative detention process.

I would be interested in your thoughts on that. Then I want to thank CBP and others. I always acknowledge the good part of their service. But I am concerned about the number of deaths, and the issues dealing with excessive force by CBP, and the report that came out that suggested that they would be engaged in reforms.

My question to you is: How will you engage to make sure those reforms move quickly, and that they are done in the highest professional way?

In addition, the CBP short-term facilities, they are at the border, and they are classified to hold 300 persons. We have found that they have held three times—that is 900 people.

A Honduran lost his life, had a massive stroke, I believe, or heart attack. He was in one of those facilities. The question is whether or not he was able to get medical care quickly enough. There are questions of heat, questions of cleanliness, et cetera.

I would be interested—we are in the business of protecting our borders. But we are also a country that believes in humanity and humaneness.

The issue of human trafficking has become a major issue in the Southern Border, in Houston, Texas. I would like to know any strategies that Homeland Security has. I have indicated we will be holding a hearing on that in Texas.

But what will Homeland Security be doing to thwart that particular issue? If you would, I would appreciate your answers. Thank you.

Secretary JOHNSON. Ma'am, first on the issue of detention, and detention practices, when I was general counsel of the Department of Defense, within the first 3 or 4 weeks I was in office, I visited our detention facilities at Guantanamo, in Iraq and Afghanistan, and urged certain reforms that were made.

I recall in Afghanistan, actually going into one of the cells, and asked the guards to close the door behind me so that I could fully understand. You could imagine the lawyer jokes when I did that. But I am very interested in this issue.

I have visited the detention center in South Texas already. I intend to visit more around the country. It is an issue that I want to study carefully.

One thing that strikes me about the Southwest Border in particular, is that almost everyone who crosses the border illegally has paid money to a smuggling organization is being trafficked, so to speak. I think the key is to attack the network in some way. In working with our inner-agency partners, working with our Mexican friends, we should focus on that.

Ms. JACKSON LEE. Thank you. I think I asked you another question about the short-term facilities and the reforms on excessive force by CBP. That is a different question. There is a report that indicated that they would be reforming their processes, as in use of force, at the border.

Secretary JOHNSON. I am very interested and concerned about use of force. I think that a law enforcement agency, foreign armed-force military, has to be credible in the communities in which it operates.

So I was happy to know that the CBP commissioner intends to make the CBP use-of-force policies public any day now. I am encouraging other components of DHS to think along those lines.

I am also interested in reviewing some of the more recent cases myself to ensure that we are getting this right.

Ms. JACKSON LEE. I think you answered the human-trafficking question about the concern by Homeland Security engaging on that issue.

Secretary JOHNSON. Yes. Yes, ma'am. It is something I intend to do.

Ms. JACKSON LEE. Thank you very much. I yield back.

Chairman MCCAUL. Let me remind Members, the Secretary has a hard stop at noon today. So I would ask that you stay within the 5-minute rule. Chairman recognizes Dr. Broun.

Mr. BROUN. Thank you, Mr. Chairman. Mr. Secretary, thank you for your statements regarding wanting to work with this committee and being responsive to our inquiries.

After years of frustration and stonewalling from your predecessor, I look forward to having a dialogue. In fact, if we had as much stonewalling going on down at the border as we have had from this administration, we would have a secure border.

I am very keen on doing that first and foremost. That being said, I am very concerned about some of your comments regarding illegal immigration.

You claim that so-called comprehensive immigration reform is a matter of homeland security, and have even gone so far as to say that those here legally have, to quote you, "earned the right to be citizens," which clearly signals that you favor amnesty.

However, as we have seen in the past, amnesty simply does not work. We need to enforce the laws on the books. We need to secure the border before any conversation on any broad reforms.

Your comments of those that you have made as well as what President Obama has made, promising amnesty, seem to encourage, not discourage, illegal entry into this country.

My question is: Do you believe that your apparent inclination towards amnesty will improve homeland security and not worsen the problem of illegal immigration?

Do you honestly believe those who have broken our laws, in fact, have broken many of our laws, including Social Security fraud, identity fraud, and lots of others, that they have earned the right to be citizens?

Secretary JOHNSON. Senator—Congressman, sorry——

Mr. BROUN. I will accept that.

Secretary JOHNSON [continuing]. The core——

[Laughter.]

Mr. BROUN. I am running for Senate.

[Laughter.]

Secretary JOHNSON [continuing]. I have spent a lot of time with Senators in the confirmation process, sorry.

The quote that you attribute to me is a misquote. That was a journalist attributing to me something I did not say.

Mr. BROUN. Okay, well, do you think that those here have earned the right to be citizens?

Do you believe——

Secretary JOHNSON. No. What I said——

Mr. BROUN [continuing]. That——

Secretary JOHNSON [continuing]. What I support is how it is reflected in the Senate bill, which was passed by a vote of 67 bipartisan Senators, which is that those present in this country, the 11.5 million or so, who go through a background check, are held accountable, who pay their taxes and do whatever the law requires them to do, should be eligible to be put on the earned path to citizenship.

Mr. BROUN. I disagree.

Let me interrupt you, sir; I apologize. I just have a very short period of time.

Secretary JOHNSON. Understood.

Mr. BROUN. I am very concerned about refugee relocation, because we are getting a lot of these refugees coming to my home State of Georgia. I am not sure that these refugees are being vetted as thoroughly as they should be.

We have a lot coming from places around the world, where there are a lot of people who want to do harm to Americans. I would like to work with you on this issue because I think this is a very dangerous issue of our accepting these refugees in this country and not having some way of monitoring them.

I think we are getting too many. These people are being forced upon American citizens in a way that is going to be dangerous for our own homeland security.

I am also very concerned about the Abu Dhabi pre-clearance that has been suggested. We have seen TSA allow people who are on the No-Fly list get on airplanes. TSA has not in itself prevented one terrorist attack.

Every single terrorist attack that we have seen on this—against this Nation, that has been prevented has not been prevented by TSA. I think TSA has been a total failure as the way it is set up now. I think we need to focus upon those who want to harm us instead of patting down Grandma and children at the airports and having this tremendous attack upon upon persons, U.S. citizens, that we need to focus on those that want to harm us, which means having the intelligence-gathering capability to focus on those and let's get rid of this idea of political correctness.

We need to focus on those that want to harm us. I don't think the Department has been. I would like very much to work with you as Secretary to try to reform or do something with TSA, to make it so that it is functional or get rid of it altogether. My time is expired.

Thank you, Mr. Chairman.

I would like to work with you as we go forward. Thank you, sir.

Chairman MCCAUL. Will the Secretary like to respond to that last—the question?

Secretary JOHNSON. Yes, just very briefly.

On the issue of refugees, I agree. We should work together on that issue. I mean, it is—when I go down to the border, it is the No. 1 thing that the people on the front line talk to me about. So I would like to work with you on that. I have some concerns.

Just on the initial point, I have told my staff we need to be more responsive to this committee and to Congress, when you write to me, when you have inquiries, I read each one personally. I have told my staff we need very prompt responses so that you get the information you need.

Mr. BROUN. I thank you for that reassurance and I look forward to working with you, sir. Thank you.

Chairman MCCAUL. The Chairman recognizes the gentleman from Arizona, Mr. Barber.

Mr. BARBER. Thank you, Mr. Chairman.

Mr. Secretary, thank you for being with us today and congratulations. I think you have taken on what I believe is the most difficult job, challenging job in the Cabinet. We all wish you well.

Our mission and your mission, I think, are united in making sure that the homeland is protected.

I also want to thank you for accepting our invitation to come down to the border less than a month after you were confirmed and sworn in. You came to my district, which is the most porous, unfortunately the most porous area of the border, where we have 13 percent of the border but have 47 percent of the pounds of drugs seized in this country. I know that the people I represent appreciate the opportunity to talk with you.

As you well know from what time we spent together, my most important priority is border security. I still have people who are unsafe on their land every single day. I still have the drugs coming in and illegal immigration is, while getting lower, still a major problem.

But my responsibility, Mr. Secretary, as you know, is to make sure that we have the resources we need, along with my colleagues, to get the job done to ensure the safety and security of people who live and work near the border. This includes steps, of course, to support our agents, our Border Patrol agents, in particular and, of course, our Customs agents, that they have the resources they need to get their job done effectively.

In January, Mr. Secretary, you issued a Department-wide memo, calling on all components to conduct a position-by-position review of the use of administratively-uncontrollable overtime or AUO. If it is found that the position uses AUO on a regular basis as a regular part of the shift duty, that position will no longer be eligible to receive AUO.

For Border Patrol agents, this policy shift threatens to reduce the number of agents or time on the border by as much as 20 percent. I believe this will undermine the progress we have made in securing our border with still work to be done.

It would also hit our Border Patrol agents and their families very hard because they would face a loss of pay due to the loss of hours, in some cases up to 20 percent pay cut.

We have heard in this committee before some reports that morale in the Federal agencies is measured and, unfortunately, the Department of Homeland Security morale is amongst the lowest. Within the Department, CBP is the lowest. I am concerned that this adjust or this change will further exacerbate the morale problem.

When we toured the border, we heard very real concerns about those who live and work near the border about the importance of ensuring safety and security 24 hours a day, 7 days a week, 365 days a year. I believe now is the time to strengthen our position and our efforts, not weaken them, as I believe this change in payment will do.

So I would like to focus my questions, Mr. Secretary, on this issue.

First of all, how do you believe that the policy is in the best interest of our security?

Should the Department and CBP decide to limit or eliminate overtime for our Border Patrol agents, what plans does it have in place to ensure that there are not big gaps in Border Patrol shifts on our U.S. borders?

Let me ask a second question and if you could answer both, there are efforts under way, Mr. Secretary, as you probably know, to reform agent pay in the AUO system; specifically, there is a bill that was introduced by Mr. Chaffetz, which I am a co-sponsor, to reform the pay system in a way that preserves security efforts and saves taxpayer money. I mean, I assume you are aware of these. If the case you are aware, why would you change the AUO system when this reform is under way?

Secretary JOHNSON. First, Congressman, thank you for spending the day with me in Arizona and introducing me to a number of State and local officials there. I appreciated the time.

With regard to AUO, as you know, we have from the Office of Special Counsel, allegations, findings, however you characterize it, of wide-spread abuse of uncontrollable overtime. The review of that is pending right now within the Department. I look forward to the results. In the interim, what was brought to us was three discrete classes of people who were eligible for AUO, that we could not continue to justify paying out AUO in that manner, given the allegations of widespread abuse. It is very—it is three very, very discrete classes of people that total, I think, 900 people across the Department of 250,000 people, just 900 people.

The suspension—and I want to emphasize this to you and to the workforce—does not affect Border Patrol agents on the front lines and people are still eligible for overtime if they earn it and they are entitled to it. They just—for those discrete number of people, they have to go through a different method to get it. But I am fully supportive of paying somebody overtime when it is necessary and when they earn it.

Mr. BARBER. Thank you, Mr. Secretary. I yield back.

Secretary JOHNSON. I am sorry. I am sorry. The bill you referred to, I am happy to review the bill.

Chairman MCCAUL. The Chairman now recognizes the Chairman of the Border and Maritime Subcommittee, Mrs. Miller.

Mrs. MILLER. Thank you very much, Mr. Chairman. I appreciate the hearing. I certainly want to, and Maritime Security as well, welcome the Secretary and thank you so much for your service to our country. We look forward to working with you.

I certainly want to add my—express my admiration as well for the great work of everybody from DHS in regards to what they did with capturing El Chapo Guzman. I certainly want to associate myself with the Chairman's very strong feelings about extradition and we appreciate your assistance, if you can help us with that as well.

As you might imagine, as a Chairman of the Border and Maritime Security Subcommittee, I have a border question. The subcommittee there, we have been working very hard on a border bill with bipartisan support, actually passed our subcommittee unanimously, and then passed the full House unanimously.

I appreciate your comments about the Senate immigration bill. However, I am one that does not agree with the Senate immigration bill, the comprehensive bill that they have passed.

However, I do think that this Congress—and I hope that we will pursue moving on a border security bill; that is one of the enumerated responsibilities under the Constitution of the Congress. I think we have to pursue that.

So I would ask you, if I could, I made a note when you were talking about establishing the metrics, that you agree with the goal of establishing metrics. Maybe you could flesh that answer out a little bit for me, if you would.

Your predecessor indicated that the term that we had used previously about establishing operational control, the term of "operational control," she said was an antiquated term.

Maybe it is, maybe it isn't. But we are trying to understand what term might be agreeable, and what the construct of those terms actually would look like.

So then we were looking at this Border Control Index. That also has been abandoned now by the DHS. But I do think it is important that we do have some actual metrics that the country can understand, that the Congress can understand, in regards to what kind of control we have at our border.

As was mentioned, about 40 percent of operational control at one point, at the Southern Border—as you know, Secretary, I am—I have a Northern Border district. That same study showed that the operational control in the Northern Border was only 4 percent. Essentially, we have no operational control on the North Border to speak of.

So could you tell us a little bit about what your Department is doing to develop measures that could give us an accurate picture, so that we could, again, understand not only our successes, but our failures as well, and so—as we can proceed on establishing border control?

Secretary JOHNSON. Let me begin by saying that in my conversations with the border-security experts in uniform, what they emphasized to me is a risk-based approach that is agile, that is not necessarily operational control, as I think a lot of people define it.

The risk-based approach is effective. It is cost-efficient. Now, in terms of metrics, I have read H.R. 1417, which defines an effectiveness rate in a certain way.

What we have said is that—well, first of all, it is Congress's prerogative to define border effectiveness, however you do that, in a fully-informed way. What we have said—and I tend to believe this—that border security should be defined by looking at a number of things. It is not simply the percentage of all those who attempt to cross the border who are either arrested or turned back. Because you have to look, first of all, at the quantity of people who are attempting to cross the border.

You have to look at the nature of the traffic. Is it third-party nationals? Is it Mexicans? Is it somebody else? You have to look at the motives, are these convicted criminals who are attempting to cross the borders for purposes of drug smuggling?

So you have to look at the nature of the traffic, the quantity of the traffic. There are a number of things which I have looked at, which I have asked my folks to further develop, that we can share with Congress in an effort to define what we believe is a secure border.

I would urge us to not focus simply on a percentage, which tends to disregard certain other very important things. So it is something that I am committed to. I think in order to further immigration reform overall, we ought to settle on a set of metrics that we all agree to and understand.

Mrs. MILLER. I appreciate that. As I am running out of time, this won't be so much a question, as just a heads-up. We will be sending you a letter on another issue about visa overstays.

Your predecessor had agreed to give the Congress a report, and the percentage of visa overstays, and how you were tracking that. That was supposed to be given to the Congress at the end of last year.

So obviously, that deadline has come and gone. We are probably going to send that letter along to you shortly, asking for that report.

Secretary JOHNSON. I have seen a draft of the report. I think it needed further work. I think that there were some things that I wanted to have some second or third opinions about before I shared it with Congress.

Mrs. MILLER. Thank you very much. Thank you, Mr. Chairman.

Chairman MCCAUL. Chairman now recognizes the gentleman from New Jersey, Mr. Payne.

Mr. PAYNE. Thank you, Mr. Chairman. Mr. Secretary, it is a real honor and a privilege to have you here today. I am just delighted that you were confirmed, and looking forward to your leadership in your capacity as Secretary, and also feel that you have one of the finest Members of Congress representing you from your district. So everyone knows, I am his constituent.

Let me just start with something that is one of my major priorities. That has been the whole issue around Sandy funding. One of my major priorities on this committee is ensuring that Hurricane Sandy relief reaches the areas that need it the most.

A portion of that funding, you know, is controlled by the State of New Jersey. I am getting disturbing complaints from constituents, from the news, from organizations like the Fair-Share Housing Center, that many municipalities that were hardest-hit, including areas where low-income and minority populations live, are not receiving the relief proportionate to the amount of damage suffered.

News reports are naturally very concerning to me. In this Congress, you know, we failed to have a hearing in reference to this. I think oversight is very important.

I was delighted to go to the floor of Congress that evening to implore my colleagues to make sure that we got the relief in that area of the country that we need it, and they responded to their fellow Americans. So even though it is my area that has benefited from that, I still feel that there needs to be oversight and responsibility to the American people, that Congress knows how those dollars are being spent, irrespective of what area it goes to.

So, you know, I am just asking—like to have you commit to ensuring that DHS is conducting proper oversight over the State of New Jersey, so that people who are deserving of that relief are being provided for.

Secretary JOHNSON. Thanks for that question, Congressman. First of all, my own home was impacted by Hurricane Sandy, took us months to repair the damage. I would also point out that a lot of the funds that we refer to when we talk about Sandy relief money is Housing and Urban Development money, as well as DHS money. There was a lot of HUD money in that mix.

I would be interested in seeing the report that you referenced. I certainly agree with the importance of Congressional oversight with regard to how the money is spent.

Mr. PAYNE. Okay. A lot of it, as you know, I think a lot of the discretion, when it comes to how that money is spent, belongs with the State?

Secretary JOHNSON. Correct.

Mr. PAYNE. But insofar as the Federal Government is concerned, I agree with you certainly about the importance of Congressional oversight.

Secretary JOHNSON. Thank you.

Mr. PAYNE. In reference to—it has been brought up on by several Members, and the Ranking Member, the whole issue around Abu Dhabi and the pre-clearance facility there. You know, I know the deputy administrator was in Abu Dhabi last week observing the operation there. There is still a lot of concern about allowing passengers, once they get here, not to be rechecked while they are in this country.

The other thing, you know, we had issues several years ago at Newark Airport, where covert operations were taking place. They were able to slip things past the TSA. So we are concerned, how often will TSA be afforded the opportunity to observe passenger screening in Abu Dhabi? Will TSA and other agents of the United States Government be allowed to conduct unannounced inspections or covert tests of the screening in Abu Dhabi?

Secretary JOHNSON. First of all, it is my understanding that the pre-clearance operations at Abu Dhabi are conducted by CBP, Customs and Border Protection. I am concerned that there not be any security gaps when it comes to arrivals as well. That is an issue that I intend to look at.

Certainly, when it comes to Newark Airport, it is an airport I am very familiar with. It is probably the airport I have used most myself. So I am concerned about security gaps, and want to focus on that, and be interested in a further dialogue with you, Congressman, on that question.

Mr. PAYNE. Okay. Thank you. I yield back.

Chairman MCCAUL. Chairman recognizes the Chairman of the Subcommittee on Cybersecurity, Infrastructure Protection, and Security Technologies, Mr. Meehan.

Mr. MEEHAN. Thank you, Mr. Chairman. Secretary, thank you for your long and distinguished service to our country. Thank you for taking on this very, very important mission. Thank you as well for the work that I know you are doing in the area of cyber. I look forward to working with you in that area as well.

But in my limited time, I want to talk about a couple of issues: One, the chemical facilities' antiterrorism standards, very important work that has been done in our country on this. We appreciate the situation in Texas, West Texas, not so long ago identifying what happens when there are outliers who are allowed to exist without our recognition of their being there.

Simultaneously or conversely, industries made significant investments in responsibly accounting for and also creating the kinds of protection systems that have been called for underneath the CFATS program. But it has now been 3 years since it has been reauthorized.

Now, there have been some breakdowns in that, to be sure, a legacy that has not been too proud from the Department. But at the same time, there has been significant progress in the course of the last year, and very deliberate efforts to look at criticisms that have been taking place, and to address those in a proactive sense.

We have introduced legislation to reauthorize the CFATS program. I want to ask whether you believe that that is a bill that you can support?

Secretary JOHNSON. I have reviewed H.R. 4007. I think it is a good bill. I am very supportive of it. Indeed, my folks tell me, "We wish we could extend the period longer."

We have a regulatory scheme that we have put in place. I agree with you, that over the last year, it has gotten better. That all stems from an appropriations measure, not an authorizations measure.

I have read this bill. I think it is a good bill. Our critical infrastructure folks think it is a good bill. I support it.

Mr. MEEHAN. Well, I thank you. I look forward to working with you. We may be able to discuss a further extension, if in fact we can make sure that we are working simultaneously towards the progression, which I think this will allow us to do.

Let me switch hats very quickly. I know you have been dealing with the questions of Abu Dhabi, so this is not a new matter for you. Although most of these decisions have been made, at least while you were overseeing your anticipated leadership.

There have been a series of programs that already exist; immigration advisory program, global entry, trusted traveler all have been used in the past. Can you explain to me whether the stated security goals that we have outlined in Abu Dhabi, could not have been realized using those kinds of programs? Or do you believe they could have been realized using the kinds of programs that currently exist, like you know, immigration advisory, et cetera, that I identified?

Secretary JOHNSON. Congressman, I think that in general, the more opportunities we have to put security in place ourselves in last points of departure airports, the better. So that bad things don't happen, not just once the terrorist gets into the country, but on the airplane, flying into the country. I have looked at the various different levels of security at our last points of departure airports. It tends to vary and that is of considerable concern to me. So, I believe—and I understand the concerns that have been raised about alternatives. I understand the concerns that have been raised from the commercial airline industry.

I believe pre-clearance is a Homeland Security imperative. Now, could things be improved at the point of arrival? Or in the Abu Dhabi situation in particular? I am not going to insist to you that, you know, we are doing it absolutely the best way. But it is a work in progress, I believe—a long road.

Mr. MEEHAN. It is just that in making those calculations—the determination to—instead of going to Dubai where we have 5 times the amount of—identified going to Abu Dhabi, did not make sense to me if in fact that was the policy?

Secretary JOHNSON. Well, Abu Dhabi is not an endpoint. I think that this is a point along the way in a progression to where I think we should get to a more aviation secure environment for this country.

Mr. MEEHAN. May I close my questioning on this? What are we going to do, as we put more resources over there and we are saying in the very airport you identified, Newark among others, as American citizens flying in from all over the world are seeing extended delays in simply getting through. You are already down in the form of resources that you need to do to work that you are doing. Why are we sending personnel overseas during a period of time when you are remarkably under-staffed right at our own border?

Secretary JOHNSON. In general, the more we can put at, you know, in forward areas, last points of departure outside this country before the terrorists can get on the airplane to fly into this country, the better. I believe that that is a Homeland Security imperative, Congressman.

Mr. MEEHAN. Mr. Chairman, I respect the 5 minutes. I yield back and look forward to working with you.

Chairman MCCAUL. Let me also say, I appreciate your support for the chemical facility anti-terrorism legislation that Mr. Meehan introduced, and as with all major legislation, I hope that we can pass that out of this committee in a bipartisan way. With that, the Chairman recognizes the gentleman from Texas, Mr. O'Rourke.

Mr. O'ROURKE. Thank you Mr. Chairman. Mr. Secretary, thank you for your comments so far and being available to answer our questions. As you have heard from other Members of the committee, I think the dominant perspective and view when it comes to our border, and certainly our border with Mexico, is to see that as a threat and a security situation to be locked down. While I think that that perspective is understandable and I think it is borne of a good intent to secure the border and secure the homeland, when you look at the facts, we are spending $18 billion a year right now, unprecedented levels of spending.

We have doubled the size of the Border Patrol in the last 10 years. We have record-low, north-bound immigration attempts, record-high south-bound deportations. El Paso, Texas, the city I have the good fortune to live in and represent, is the safest city in America today, 4 years in a row actually, bordering on Ciudad Juarez, the largest—with what is the largest bi-national community in the world. San Diego is in the top 10 safest cities, Laredo is in the top 10 safest cities, Honolulu, another port city, is among the top 10 safest cities. So, I want to hear you talk about the opportunities at the border?

In El Paso alone, we have 22 million pedestrian and auto crossings every single year. It is the lifeblood of our economy and it is the lifeblood of who we are as a community. That is in addition to the $90 billion in U.S.-Mexico trade that passed through there. That trade, that commerce, and that human crossing activity support more than 400,000 jobs in the State of Texas, more than 6 million in the United States at large, and yet those ports of entry in El Paso, in Arizona, other parts of the U.S.-Mexico border, are sorely understaffed. What is your proposal and plan to make sure that we have the resources to capitalize on the opportunities at the U.S.-Mexico border?

Secretary JOHNSON. In this job, Secretary of Homeland Security, it has been made very clear to me that part of my mission is to facilitate and expedite trade. Whether it is on the Southwest Border or the Northern Border. You know, for example, the Canadians have talked to me about our bridge crossings in Michigan and the importance of building—funding a Customs plaza on the U.S. side in Michigan. Same with Texas, with south Texas, where I was a couple of weeks ago. I haven't been to El Paso yet, but I hope to go there soon. But, it has been stressed to me the importance of, as a matter of Customs enforcement, facilitating and promoting trade.

Now, that also depends on Congress being willing to fund at the appropriate levels, our Customs plazas, our ability on the U.S. side of a bridge or a land port to be—you know to build these things. So we need Congress to authorize and appropriate. But I want to work with you on that, and I recognize the importance of promoting trade. Whether it is El Paso, or Detroit, or any of our other ports of entry.

Mr. O'ROURKE. I appreciate that answer, and I will do my part as a Member of Congress, to make sure that we have those resources there. But even within the existing DHS budget, I just urge you to deploy those resources and assets as intelligently and as effectively as possible to capitalize on those opportunities that we have there.

I want to associate myself with Mr. Barber's remarks earlier about supporting our men and women in the Border Patrol. They have among the toughest jobs that I can imagine. The level of vigilance required, the terrain that they are working within, the encounters that they have to deal with.

So I also join him in urging you to support Mr. Chaffetz's bill to make sure that we have some fairness and predictability when it comes to pay for the members of the Border Patrol. But I also want to make sure that we have the appropriate oversight and accountability for law enforcement on the border. I appreciate the fact that you are going to release the CBP's Use of Force Policy. I would also ask you to release the Police Executive Research Forum's report on CBP's use of force. Right now, we only know about these use of force incidents anecdotally. I get them in my office regularly, and I also hear far too often from these 22 million bridge-crossers, a lack of respect, and sometimes poor treatment and sometimes abuse at the hands of CBP Officers on our border.

We need greater oversight and accountability given the missions and the opportunities there at the border. So, I would just ask you to release that. Also as one of the other Members of the committee said, become more transparent and accountable as an agency. I think that has been a major failing of DHS up until now.

Secretary JOHNSON. I will look at this particular report you refer to, Congressman. I agree generally with the importance of law enforcement being credible, and being transparent in the communities in which they operate. If law enforcement—and you see this also in the military context, is viewed with suspicion, is not credible, it undermines the entire mission.

Mr. O'ROURKE. Great. I appreciate that. Thank you very much. Thank you Mr. Chairman.

Chairman MCCAUL. The Chairman recognizes the Chairman of the Subcommittee on Oversight and Management Efficiency, Mr. Duncan.

Mr. DUNCAN. Thank you Mr. Chairman and thanks for this hearing. Secretary Johnson, thanks for being here, and I am impressed with what I have seen so far, and I look forward to working with you on an on-going basis.

In your statement, you talked about being responsive to inquiries and letters from Members and committees of Congress. I just want to bring one example to your attention. June 16—June 6, 2013 letter to Under Secretary Borras dealing with training videos that has never been answered. I will make sure my staff gets your guys a copy of that so that it can be answered.

Secretary JOHNSON. Happy to do that, sir.

Mr. DUNCAN. Yes, thank you. Thank you for that. Because I think that is important. That is part of the oversight function. Oftentimes we can't have hearings, but we can send direct inquiries to the agencies and the departments for request of information. I sat here earlier thinking about all of the things you are responsible for. It is sort of overwhelming. Border security, immigration, customs enforcement, USCIS, maritime and port security, the Coast Guard, transportation security, air security, Secret Service, law enforcement training, cyber threats, FEMA, and all of the things that our committee deals with. That is a tremendous responsibility that you have to keep this Nation safe.

I just want to make sure that the folks watching at home understand the Department of Homeland Security brought 22 agencies together, our sub-agencies, under one umbrella. In the last decade or a little more, trying to make sure that all of those operate in a very cohesive fashion. So, I fully understand the challenge. I just want to go on the record for that.

I want to shift gears and talk about something that is on my mind regularly as we talk about immigration reform. Because the numbers that were used today, roughly 11.5 million—say 12 million illegal immigrants in the United States. Roughly 40 to 49 percent of those didn't just violate our sovereignty by crossing our border—Southern Border, Northern Border, doesn't matter.

They actually violated the National trust that we have placed in them. Because we gave them a permission slip to come here, known as a visa. Where they had an interview at a consulate or an embassy and we have the correct spelling of their name. We have got a picture, probably a fingerprint. We know where they were going in most instances. We know they were going to work, or coming to school. Tourists? I get that, that they could travel just about anywhere. But, we have got an address of where a lot of these folks were going. Where they were going to work, or where they were going to attend college. Roughly half of the illegals in this country, I estimated 4.8 million to 5.8 million people that are here illegally, overstayed their visa. They didn't just cross the border. We gave them a permission slip to come into this country, and they violated our trust. This is low-hanging fruit from a customs and immigration enforcement issue. So the question I have for you is, don't you think that we should work real hard, because the information that I have—that ICE devotes less than 2 percent of its investigative resources investigating these overstays. Less than 2 percent, but we know who these people are.

This isn't chasing a footprint in the desert. So don't you think we ought to ramp up that percentage, put more effort in effectively enforcing the immigration laws that we have with regard to these overstays, either getting them back into a legal status if they are still attending college somewhere or still gainfully employed, but deal with half these illegals before we take on a whole 'nother avenue of immigration enforcement?

So I would love to hear your thoughts with regard to these overstays, enforcement policies, and dedication of ICE resources to investigating these.

Secretary JOHNSON. First of all, I don't know that the number is 40 percent. Forty percent has kind of worked into the narrative based on a report that was done some years ago. It is my understanding that is not a Government report.

I don't know that it is 40 percent.

Mr. DUNCAN. Well, use whatever percentage we want, 20 percent, 25 percent, 30 percent, 15 percent, it doesn't matter to me. It still remains that this is low-hanging fruit of information we know about these people. We know who they are. So I will——

Secretary JOHNSON. I do agree that we should correlate resources to the removal of—and the way in which we say we ought to prioritize my removals. In my view, as a matter of homeland security, we need to prioritize our removals with regard to National security, public safety, border security threats, as a matter of homeland security.

If in the category of visa overstays there are those people we need to focus on going after those people——

Mr. DUNCAN. They are a National security threat. So——

Secretary JOHNSON [continuing]. Public safety threats, which involve those convicted of serious crimes and border security threats, you know, people who are recent border crossers who are apprehended in and around the border, who are repeat crossers and the like, the people who represent threats to border security.

I agree entirely with your point that we ought to correlate resources with our priorities. We've got to devote the resources to meet what we say should be the priorities. My priorities are homeland security, protecting the American people, enforcing our immigration laws. We need to correlate our resources in that way.

Mr. DUNCAN. Thank you for that. I will just remind the committee, I believe that 7 of the 10 hijackers on 9/11 had overstayed a visa.

I yield back.

Secretary JOHNSON. I understand your point.

Chairman MCCAUL. The Chairman will now recognize the gentlelady from Hawaii, Ms. Gabbard.

Ms. GABBARD. Thank you very much, Mr. Chairman.

Welcome and aloha, Secretary. Great to have you here with us.

You have touched on a lot of different topics today that I look forward to being able to address that really impact us Nationally from cyber threats to domestic drone use and the policies that we need to come up with as we look at this new technology, duplication of resources, aging Coast Guard fleet, and so on and so forth.

I also want to welcome you to come and visit Hawaii. I know you have been there before, but to come in this capacity, because there is nothing like seeing first-hand the challenges as well as the opportunities that we have that are unique from the rest of the country, from the District 14 Coast Guard, which covers, by far, the largest sector of any district that the Coast Guard has responsibility over, and the unique implications of what they do on the international front, engagement, diplomacy, the exclusive economic zones that they patrol, it is really quite impactful what they are responsible for and how they have done so well with such little resources.

Also just to touch on the portal that exists in our State, both the air portal and the international port are really being the gateway between Asia and the United States as well as in our maritime ports.

Since 1996, we have had two international airports in the State of Hawaii, the primary, which is the Honolulu International Airport and the Kona International Airport.

Kona was able to accept flights and we had Customs and Border Patrol operating from there up until 2011. This is a situation I know that you are familiar with and that we are trying to remedy. The CBP has stated basically that the facilities at the Kona airport were insufficient in 2011. The airport facility staff sought feedback from CBP in 2012, were given a book of regulations, 295 pages, that was dated in 2006, told to look through it and update the facility.

The following year, they were given an updated book in 2011, said, oh, well, this is the updated version.

I think our folks on the ground have been really proactive in trying to make sure that we are able to meet CBP standards and are requesting a 5-year exemption so that we can continue to operate as we were up until 2011, which is important from an economic perspective, but also from a security perspective, if anything were to happen at the Honolulu International Airport, that we have another gateway and we have another facility there.

So I am wondering if you can comment on the status of that request that is supported by the mayor on the ground as well as by the Governor.

Secretary JOHNSON. I have your letter in this regard. I will probably get myself into trouble by saying that I have been to Kona Airport and it is probably the most pleasant airport experience I have had in a very long time. It is a very—I also—I recall that when you can fly from Kona to the mainland, and I don't think it was in the early 1990s. I am not sure you can do that anymore.

Ms. GABBARD. You can.

Secretary JOHNSON. I know the burden of being on a multi-hour flight to Honolulu and then you got to change planes and fly to Kona. So I know the inconvenience of that.

So I would like to see us work with local airport officials to try to get to a place where you can have an international arrivals capability. I am—you know, you make a good point, that if you lose one you don't have a second.

So I would like to see us try to work together on that. I do believe, however, that we can't do something that is going to potentially compromise aviation security, Border Patrol security, and so I am personally familiar with the Kona airport. Happy to try to work with your constituents, represent local officials in this regard, to get there with the concern for security.

Ms. GABBARD. Thank you. I appreciate being able to work with you on that. Understand that the private sector is also very much invested in helping to bring this about. Applied for a reimbursable agreement, was denied by CBP, and hope to become one of the other cities that will be approved at some point in the future.

I want to touch quickly on airline fees with the budget that was passed recently, some of these fees that directly impact airline travel were increased in part to help pay for CBP to help pay for TSA. I am going to be an advocate here for the two non-contiguous States, Hawaii and Alaska, where air travel is essentially our only option. This is not an area that is a luxury, but one that is essential for business, for health care, for education and look forward to working with you on seeing how we can, as has been done in the past, make sure that these two States are considered differently.

Secretary JOHNSON. I have your bill in this regard. I have read your bill. You know, I am interested in studying it further.

Ms. GABBARD. Thank you very much.

Thank you, Mr. Chairman.

Chairman MCCAUL. The Chairman recognizes the gentleman from Utah, Mr. Chaffetz.

Mr. CHAFFETZ. Oh, thank you, Mr. Chairman.

Thank you and congratulations, Mr. Secretary. I look forward to working with you. I think you properly pointed out in your testimony that people are your greatest asset.

One of the areas of concern that I have is how do we do security clearances, background checks on the personnel? The overwhelming majority of people, good quality people; I do have questions and concerns as I highlighted in a letter more than 2 weeks ago about your current chief of staff, Mr. Christian Marrone.

When and where did you first meet Christian Marrone?

Secretary JOHNSON. First of all, I have your letter. You asked that I respond by the 26th, which is today, and I will be responding today.

Mr. CHAFFETZ. Thank you.

Secretary JOHNSON. In a timely fashion.

I first met Mr. Marrone in early 2009 at the Department of Defense.

Mr. CHAFFETZ. Was there a background check conducted on Mr. Marrone before the appointment you made to his being the chief of staff?

Secretary JOHNSON. You mean chief of staff for DHS?

Mr. CHAFFETZ. Yes.

Secretary JOHNSON. Yes, to the best of my understanding, there was.

I also know him for 5 years and know his qualities. I am glad I hired him.

Mr. CHAFFETZ. So there was a background check. Did you review that background check?

Secretary JOHNSON. Not myself, no.

Mr. CHAFFETZ. Who did read it?

Secretary JOHNSON. The appropriate officials, I am quite sure. My understanding is that the background check was quite thorough, which included matters of public record from the Fumo trial, which is what your letter refers to.

Mr. CHAFFETZ. Did the White House review it?

Secretary JOHNSON. So far as I know, they did.

Mr. CHAFFETZ. Were there any——

Secretary JOHNSON. As is the standard practice.

Mr. CHAFFETZ. Did it reveal any concerns?

Secretary JOHNSON. Mr. Marrone's background was viewed extensively, including the matters of public record. I have every reason to believe that it was thorough, and we hired him, and I am glad we did. He is doing an excellent job for the Department.

Mr. CHAFFETZ. Who conducted the background check?

Secretary JOHNSON. I could not tell you that, sir.

Mr. CHAFFETZ. Are you aware of any court judgments against Mr. Marrone?

Secretary JOHNSON. Not sitting here right now, no.

Mr. CHAFFETZ. When did you become aware of the trial involving Pennsylvania State Senator Vincent Fumo?

Secretary JOHNSON. In 2008.

Mr. CHAFFETZ. Did you—when did you first become aware of Christian Marrone and his testifying in the trial involving Vincent Fumo?

Secretary JOHNSON. In 2009.

Mr. CHAFFETZ. Did you review, are you aware of the city of Philadelphia's forensic review and financial investigation into three of the entities that Mr. Marrone was involved and engaged in?

Secretary JOHNSON. Not specifically, no, sir, but I would like to say that I hired Mr. Marrone because he was working for Robert Gates and Robert Rangel in the front office of the Secretary of Defense. Those two individuals are demanding, scrupulous people who expect the highest of people.

Mr. Marrone impressed me while we worked together at DOD for his administrative organizational skills, his ability to put together a budget process, and his ability to identify inefficiencies.

I hired him at DHS to do the same there. He is doing an excellent job. He is doing the job that I think Members of Congress would want us all to do for the Department.

Mr. CHAFFETZ. Were you aware when you selected Mr. Marrone to be your chief of staff at Homeland Security that he made personal use of moneys from tax-exempt charities?

Secretary JOHNSON. I was generally aware of his public testimony. It was highly-publicized and it concerned events 12–17 years ago. I am more focused on the last 5 years, when he has worked in National security.

Mr. CHAFFETZ. Were you aware when he was hired that, at one time, he secured in writing from Mr. Fumo approval for the retention of a private investigator to "snoop" on then-mayor of Philadelphia, Ed Rendell?

Secretary JOHNSON. As I said, his employment by Senator Fumo, 12 to 17 years ago, when he was in his early 20s, is a matter of public record. It was highly publicized. Anybody who knows Christian Marrone knows that when he came out of college, 12–17 years ago, he worked for Senator Fumo.

If you don't, you could figure that out by spending 6 seconds on the internet.

Mr. CHAFFETZ. That is exactly my concern is that he has been engulfed in a variety of controversy.

Have you reviewed this e-mail that Christian sent, this is on April 21, back in 1998, concerned about the Department must change its practices of hiring. He is referring to the Philadelphia Police Department, where he says, "The end result has been the skipping over of qualified white candidates and the hiring of minorities with criminal records."

He wants—he advocates changing the city charter, and again, goes on—I will give you the full e-mail, if you haven't seen it, "The result is an uneducated, unskilled, and unqualified department of minority officers."

I would think that this would cause concern in addition to all the public things that are out there about Mr. Fumo; I would encourage you to please look at the public record regarding judgments.

My time has expired, Mr. Chairman.

But I do hope to chat with you on this. I was disappointed when I asked if I could come see you personally and talk to you about this, I was told no. I couldn't do that.

Secretary JOHNSON. I actually was told that you wanted to talk to me. I said, yes, I am happy to talk to the Congressman. But for some reason, you were unavailable.

I am happy to talk to you further about this issue.

Mr. CHAFFETZ. I would love to come sit down with you and talk to you about it. I have great concerns about this.

Secretary JOHNSON. May I respond, sir?

Chairman McCAUL. Yes, Mr. Secretary,

Secretary JOHNSON. Congressman, I am focused on trying to make the Department of Homeland Security a more efficient and effective place for the benefit of the public, for the benefit of the taxpayers.

I have known Mr. Marrone since 2009, when he worked for Robert Gates. Secretary Gates held him in the highest regard. I hired him to be our chief of staff because of his organizational administrative skills over the last 5 years, that had been demonstrated to a lot of people.

Since he has come to the Department of Homeland Security, my expectations for him have been, in fact, exceeded.

This is a man who has three young children. He is married. He is at work at 5 a.m. He is streamlining our organization. He is making the Department of Homeland Security a more efficient place.

He is putting together a budget process, something that people on this committee and in this Congress have been after us to do for some years.

He is doing an excellent job for the benefit of the public and the taxpayer.

Mr. CHAFFETZ. Mr. Chairman, I appreciate the excess time.

But three of the entities he was involved with, the inspector general of the city of Philadelphia said was fraudulent, misrepresented, misspent money, and overspent some $5-million-plus that they want to get back in the city of Philadelphia. That is the concern.

Chairman McCAUL. The gentleman's time has expired.

We have 10 Members left. The Secretary has agreed to stay until 12:15. So I would ask unanimous consent that all Members limit their questions to 3 minutes, so we can accommodate all the Members.

The gentleman from California, Mr. Swalwell.

Mr. SWALWELL. Thank you, Mr. Chairman.

Thank you, Mr. Secretary, for being here today. Welcome. We do look forward to your leadership.

Secretary JOHNSON. Thank you.

Mr. SWALWELL. A quick question about the Urban Area Security Initiative program, known as UASI. The Department develops a risk score for UASIs by looking at factors like population, military assets, critical infrastructure, et cetera.

But some UASIs fund additional counties and neighboring areas that have close economic and military ties that are in the commute areas.

For example, in the Bay Area, where I am from, San Francisco, we have 5 of the—we have 12 counties, but 5 are not included in our Urban Areas Initiative grant.

We are wondering and hoping if the Department can work with us to consider other assets and population and cultural and economic ties to bring into the Bay Area's footprint some of these surrounding counties, because they do include Travis Air Force Base, the Defense Language Institute, and a number of other important assets.

Secretary JOHNSON. I am very familiar with the Bay Area and all that it includes. I have spent considerable time in the Bay Area. I am happy to take a look at this issue and work with you more on it.

Mr. SWALWELL. Great.

The second question, with respect to immigration enforcement priorities, I know, being a former prosecutor, that how you classify different crimes is important. Right now, 72 percent of individuals removed were convicted of Level 1 or Level 2 offenses. A Level 1 offense can include an aggravated felony, and a Level 2 offense can include multiple misdemeanors, which also could be driving without a license, which, of course, if an undocumented person is here, they would not be able to obtain a license.

I want to make sure that we are focusing on removing the most serious and violent offenders, and not necessarily breaking up families that are—especially my concern, being a former prosecutor, was people would commit crimes that were—we would call it a crime for driving without a license, but, up until just a couple months ago in California, an undocumented person could never receive a license.

So were you focused on more violent individuals when we prioritize removal?

Secretary JOHNSON. I am committed—and I am continuing a continual evaluation and reevaluation of our prosecution priorities and ensuring that we are operating and acting in accordance with those.

So it is something that I am going to continually look at.

Mr. SWALWELL. Great.

With that, Mr. Chairman, I will yield back the balance of my time.

Again, thank you so much, Mr. Secretary. We look forward to working with you.

Chairman MCCAUL. The Chairman recognizes the Chairman of the Subcommittee on Transportation Security, Mr. Hudson from North Carolina.

Mr. HUDSON. Thank you, Mr. Chairman.

Mr. Secretary, thank you for being with us here today.

I am extremely concerned and upset about the cost, overall cost, and the delays of the new Department of Homeland Security headquarters at St. Elizabeth's campus.

The cost has now ballooned to something like $4.5 billion. A completion date has moved out from 2015 to 2026. Frankly, I just fail to see how this is an appropriate use of the taxpayer dollars, to spend this kind of money for a headquarters, and just really disappointed in the way it has played out.

You know, I understand, when you are consolidating 22 agencies, this is a very difficult process. I understand the command-and-control concerns of having your agency scattered all across the region.

But to put this in perspective, the world's tallest building only cost a billion dollars and it only took a fraction of the time to build.

Frankly, I think the way we are going about this, by trying to take these historic buildings that are crumbling and trying to bring them up to speed and build a facility is the wrong way to go.

I mean, I am a history major, so I am trying to contemplate or even comprehend this type of money. You talk about $4 billion, it is a quarter of the amount of money we spent to rebuild Japan after World War II, and it is 3 years longer.

I was doing some math, and $4 billion, if you were to stack dollar bills, would be as tall as a thousand Empire State Buildings.

I mean, this is an incredible amount of money for a headquarters when we have got so many other needs in Homeland Security and other things, when we are borrowing 40 cents of every dollar we spend.

I realize that decisions were made on these headquarters before your tenure and, frankly, before I got here. So, my question to you is: Will you be willing to work with us? Can you go back to the drawing board and let's come up with a better plan that doesn't cost us $4.5 billion to meet the needs of the Department?

Secretary JOHNSON. I have asked my folks to work with GSA on a plan going forward.

My general observations about St. Elizabeth's: First of all, it is a wonderful place. The Coast Guard is headquartered there now.

It is a terrific place. I am envious. But I will probably never work there.

From my Pentagon experience, I do believe there is a value for the, you know, "One Team, One Mission" message, if you have all the components in one headquarters. I have seen that at the Pentagon.

In the E-Ring, you have got DOD. You have got Army, Navy, Air Force, Marine Corps, all in the same square footage. There is value to that.

I think that the morale of DHS, unity of the mission, that emphasis would go a long way if we could get to a headquarters.

I also believe we ought to finish what we started. You know, we are investing a lot of money in this project. There is a certain wisdom to finishing what you start. Then the question becomes the time line pursuant to which you finish it. So, we have got some years ahead of us.

But I have asked my folks to work with GSA. So I have some of the same questions you do.

Mr. HUDSON. I appreciate that. I know I am out of time, but finish what you started. If you are in the middle of a huge mess, you stop digging. We are in the middle of a boondoggle of epic proportions. I would just say we need to look at starting over.

We could build a skyscraper up on that mountain, and put the whole Government in it for that kind of money.

Let's look at a new plan.

But I look forward to working with you.

Chairman MCCAUL. The gentleman's time is expired. I now recognize Mr. Higgins.

Mr. HIGGINS. Thank you, Mr. Chairman.

Mr. Secretary, I just wanted to get back to the Northern Border and security. I represent Buffalo, and we have the Peace Bridge. It connects Buffalo to southern Ontario, which is a population center of 8 million people.

Secretary JOHNSON. Sorry I couldn't be there Monday.

Mr. HIGGINS. What is that?

Secretary JOHNSON. Sorry I couldn't be there Monday.

Mr. HIGGINS. You were missed. But it was a good event, and we are making progress.

It is the second-busiest Northern Border crossing between the United States and Canada. Forty billion dollars in trade crosses the bridge every year.

In previous hearings here, on Hezbollah, which is a Shia terrorist organization bent on violent jihad, it was disclosed that Hezbollah has a presence in North America, including 15 American cities and two major cities in Canada.

In the post-9/11 era, the one thing we know clearly is that terrorists seek to destruct and kill, but they also seek to disrupt our way of life. So they seek out high-impact targets.

Around the Peace Bridge—we have no other Peace Bridge. As I said, second-busiest Northern Border cross between the United States and Canada, but also Niagara Falls, destination of some 20 million visitors from every country in the world, every year. A high-impact target.

The Niagara Power project produces the largest, the most hydroelectricity in all of New York State. A high-impact target.

Toronto, an international city, a high-impact target.

Earlier, last year, a terrorist plot was thwarted that was targeting a passenger train from Niagara Falls to New York City.

So I just wanted to make you aware of that and get your thoughts on it quickly. Thank you.

Secretary JOHNSON. Thank you for that, Congressman.

I am aware that some of the most serious border threats can be threats to the Northern Border. They are of a different character and kind from the threats on the Southwest Border. I appreciate that.

I also recognize the importance of facilitating trade in places like the Peace Bridge and I know that you and Senator Schumer and others have been very focused on that and I congratulate you for those efforts.

The Northern Border is one I expect to get to very soon in my travels so I can study this issue further. I agree with your concerns regarding security.

Mr. HIGGINS. Thank you. With that, I yield back.

Chairman MCCAUL. I thank the gentleman for yielding back time. Chairman now recognizes the gentleman from Pennsylvania, Mr. Barletta.

Mr. BARLETTA. Thank you, Mr. Chairman and thank you Mr. Secretary for coming here today. As was noted earlier, today is the 21st anniversary of the 1993 World Trade Center bombings as you well know.

Mahmud Abouhalima is one of the terrorists who perpetrated this attack. He overstayed a tourist visa and received amnesty when comprehensive immigration reform was passed in 1986. He claimed that he was really a cab driver, but he claimed to be a seasonal agricultural worker. The only thing he ever planted in America was a bomb.

Terrorists in this country need to find a way to remain here legally and not be deported. It is possible and likely that there are people in this country illegally who have connections to radical groups in the Middle East.

Secretary Johnson, my question is that employees within the DHS say that they are pressured to rubber-stamp citizenship and visa applications and lack the resources to adequately investigate applicants.

I was a mayor, and I am very aware of what is involved in doing criminal background checks. If we do not conduct face-to-face interviews in these background checks, how can we be sure that we are not gonna legalize individuals who have connections to radical groups in the Middle East as any part of any immigration reform that is being discussed here?

You know again, I have seen the other side of illegal immigration. I know we talk a lot about, you know, the good people who are here just working. But, you know, I have seen the criminal aspect and the drug dealers.

How are are you going to separate salt from sugar if we are not going to do face-to-face interviews and investigate the backgrounds of these people and their country of origin?

Secretary JOHNSON. First of all, Congressman, thank you for that question.

When it comes to counter-terrorism, I don't think I take a back seat to anybody, and I think my track record in National security demonstrates that. I am most concerned about identifying individuals of suspicion who have terrorist motives in this country or who want to come into this country.

Regarding the complaint that some may feel pressure to rubber-stamp a visa application, I have heard this before. It is something I have asked about. I have asked my folks to look into it. I am interested in the subject and it is something that I am willing to engage with your office about so that we can both understand the nature of it.

Mr. BARLETTA. Could you address the face-to-face interviews? How are we going to conduct background checks on any immigration reform without doing those type of very, very time-consuming——

Secretary JOHNSON. I have asked the same question, so.

Mr. BARLETTA. I would like to work with you if we can, I am very concerned.

Secretary JOHNSON. Yes.

Mr. BARLETTA. Thank you.

Chairman MCCAUL. The Chairman now recognizes the gentleman from Nevada, Mr. Horsford. Mr. Horsford.

Mr. HORSFORD. Thank you, Mr. Chairman, I will be brief.

Mr. Secretary, thank you for being here today. Earlier this week I had the opportunity to meet with my sheriff from Clark County, as well as our fire chief and 12 local first responders from agencies throughout Southern Nevada.

During this meeting, they expressed concern that the current risk-assessment model does not factor in considerations that are unique to tourism-centered locations such as Las Vegas and that the model seems to be moving more to a response and recovery approach and not as much a focus on prevention.

The Attorney General, Eric Holder, who has visited this southern Nevada fusion center considers it to be the model for how agencies should be working together.

The officials with whom I met believe that they were not sufficiently involved in the risk evaluation process and that FEMA did not take advantage of their local expertise as first responders.

Now, I know these concerns apply to other cities throughout the country, beyond Las Vegas in the last year, including places like Orlando and New Orleans who have also fallen off the UASI list.

But I also know that you have inherited this model. So as you lay the foundation for this new Department of Homeland Security under your administration, I would like to ask for your commitment to work with me and other colleagues on addressing issues with the risk assessment model that does not adequately factor the unique characterizations and needs of tourism-based economies like the one I represent.

I want to personally invite you out to our community to meet with our Fusion Center representative as well as the public and private sector who have concerns about the fact that we have moved away from this focus on prevention.

I want to ask if you will review that model, going forward, and if you will take me up on my invitation to come to Las Vegas.

Secretary JOHNSON. You are correct that I have inherited the model, but I now own it, so it is mine. I have heard this issue before, and not just from a Congressional representative in Nevada and I am willing to review it, work with you on it to make sure we have gotten it right.

I understand the concerns around potential threat to tourism, so I get that.

Mr. HORSFORD. Thank you. Again, I would like to——

Secretary JOHNSON. I would welcome the opportunity to visit Nevada again.

Mr. HORSFORD. Thank you. Yes, the Fusion Center is a great place and again, I think it is a model as the Attorney General Eric Holder has said for how local State and Federal agencies, public, private entities can work together to proactively meet our security needs.

Thank you, Mr. Chairman.

Chairman MCCAUL. The gentleman from Pennsylvania, Mr. Perry, is recognized.

Mr. PERRY. Thank you, Mr. Chairman. Mr. Secretary, welcome and congratulations, you have got a tough job.

Recently, a DHS drone was used to assist local law enforcement in apprehending a North Dakota man after a dispute with some cattle.

It is my understanding the drones are to be used to assist in the apprehension of illegal immigrants who cross the border, not for domestic surveillance of American citizens.

Also, in 2014, we appropriated almost a billion dollars towards CBP's Office of Air and Maritime, which includes unmanned aircraft operations for the robust airborne intelligence, surveillance, and reconnaissance to extend the reach of CBP's drug interdiction and border security operation.

Not to indict you for the sins of the past and your predecessor, but there were often cries that the Department or—didn't have enough money, didn't have the funds to carry out its mission.

I am wondering if—two things—if this is going to continue the use of DHS drones for law enforcement regarding American citizens? If it does—and if it is, then shouldn't we consider the budget in that regard and, you know, are you really that short in funds if you are using the asset that had been appropriated for the Department for specific reasons and then is used elsewhere for local law enforcement?

Then how do you know, are you going to continue that policy? Then how do you determine—I mean, maybe the community I represent is interested in using DHS drone for law enforcement, but how do we get in the queue then?

So, just like to get some of your thoughts on——

Secretary JOHNSON. My general comment is this: I think that surveillance, including aerial surveillance, is very important for border security. Border security is one of my missions.

I want to be sure, as we go forward with this technology that we are also providing adequate assurances, safeguards, protections, when it comes to the privacy of our citizens who live in and around the border.

I want to be sure we further refine our policies in that regard if we are going to continue to conduct surveillance along the border.

With regard to your specific question about uses for law enforcement and funding, I would have to get back to you on that. But my general view is that there is an important need for surveillance for purposes of border security and that is my primary——

Mr. PERRY. I agree with you, and I don't want to interrupt you. But I have got just a few moments left.

The Washington Times reported that the DHS had lent border drones out to local State and Federal agencies hundreds of times, so I just want to—and so that is domestic—that surveillance of American citizens, is it generally your theme, or something that you would accept that you would continue in that regard?

I am asking from privacy standpoint, from a legality standpoint and from a funding standpoint, is the Department going to continue to do that?

Secretary JOHNSON. Look, my principle—my priority is border security, that is part of the homeland security mission. That is my priority.

If I have surveillance technology that Congress has funded and given to me for that purpose, that is my priority.

Mr. PERRY. For Americans or for people on the border that are coming——

Secretary JOHNSON. For border security. For——

Mr. PERRY. Only?

Secretary JOHNSON [continuing]. Border crossings, I can't say solely, there may be some instances where for a very important law enforcement objective, we might support some local law enforcement's efforts at drug trafficking or something of that nature. So I wouldn't rule that out.

But the principle reason they are there is border security.

Mr. PERRY. Thank you.

Chairman McCAUL. The gentleman's time has expired.

Gentlelady from New York, Ms. Clarke.

Ms. CLARKE. Thank you very much, Mr. Chairman, and welcome Mr. Secretary. I am going to just give you my questions and then have you respond, given the time constraint.

It is good to hear that you support the CFATS legislation. It is my understanding, however, that DHS is currently engaged in a working group whose recommendations will be coming out in May. So I just want to get your feedback as to whether you think it would be great for us to be informed by what the working group comes out with as we move forward to bring forth legislation.

I also want to raise the issue of personnel surety. This is a—the direction that NYPD is going with components of CFATS raises some issues of long-standing concerns to this committee.

Lack of standardization and harmonization in the area of personal surety requirements across critical infrastructure sectors. If you would address that.

Then, finally, just a comment. I want to applaud you on your commitment to comprehensive immigration reform and add my voice to encourage you to prioritize those who we are looking at in terms of their immigrant status when we are looking at removals. That—if we can drill down into the agency to look at that categorization, because I believe that comprehensive immigration reform is inevitable. The status quo just can't hold. But, we are also dealing with the fragmentation of families, and oftentimes the breadwinners of those families.

Having said that, I look forward to your response, sir.

Secretary JOHNSON. Yes ma'am, first my general attitude is if we have got a good bill and there is an opportunity to pass it in this

Congress that supports my goals and objectives, enhances home-land security, I am going to support that measure.

If there is support for it, it is a good bill—I think we in the Congressional and Executive branches owe it to the American people to try to get something done. So that is my general attitude and I think that this bill is a good bill.

I believe we need to continually evaluate our removal priorities to make sure we are getting it right, the removal—border threats are—you know, it is a fluid situation. You have to continually re-evaluate it and that is what I am doing.

I am sorry that I have forgotten your second question.

Ms. CLARKE. Yes, it was about the personnel surety program.

Right now, we are dealing with an issue of background checks and credentials across several agencies and the redundancy of that. Would you give us your——

Secretary JOHNSON. I am very interested in achieving greater efficiencies and that is a directive that I have given to my staff to look for, whether it is with regard to background checks or a number of other items.

Ms. CLARKE. Thank you.

Chairman MCCAUL. Gentlelady's time is expired.

Mrs. Brooks.

Mrs. BROOKS. Thank you, Secretary for being here and for sitting here even longer than you were expected.

In the past two budget cycles, the President's proposed consolidating several of the Homeland Security grant programs administered by FEMA into a National preparedness grant program, but that request has been denied by—in a bicameral, bipartisan way, because there were never enough details provided as to how this was going to affect our State and local partners. We are still waiting and have been waiting to hear what FEMA proposed with respect to consolidating these very important grant programs.

I am curious whether or not you have seen the language, whether or not the administration is planning on submitting this consolidated grant program once again?

I have one other quick question for you.

Secretary JOHNSON. I will have to get back to you on that one. Sorry.

Mrs. BROOKS. Okay, I would just let you know that it has been met with much opposition by both sides, both chambers, and would expect it to receive the same response if it is presented in the same way.

We also, in sharing the Emergency Preparedness Response Communication Subcommittee, we just held a hearing recently on the bio-terror threat facing the country. You may or may not be aware, but the Weapons of Mass Destruction Center issued a report card that showed that we, in this country, received grades of a large number of Ds and Fs in our preparation for a bio-terror threat.

Wasn't—would like to know—one of the recommendations out of the 112th Congress was that the Next Generation–3 system that was proposed for detecting bio-terrorism exceeded cost by almost three times, to $5.8 billion in the life cycle for the—what is called Gen3 of the Bio-Watch program.

Did not know if you have been yet briefed on the Bio-Watch program, the analysis of alternatives, and whether or not you were aware that our country really is lacking in its preparedness and its response for a bio-terror attack.

Secretary JOHNSON. Bio-terror—the bio-terror threat is part of the Homeland Security mission. It is—on my watch I have been briefed generally on the bio-terror concerns that we all have, and agree that this has got to be a real priority in a cost-effective way. I am happy to work with you, further the dialogue on this and make sure we address this in a cost-efficient, effective way.

Mrs. BROOKS. I just might make a suggestion that came out during this hearing, that there is currently no one singular person that has his or her mission in Department of Homeland Security to be responsible for bio-terror. I would encourage you to look at that. It is—there have been those positions in past administrations. There currently is not that in this administration.

Thank you.

Chairman MCCAUL. Gentlelady's time has expired.

Mr. Richmond, from Louisiana.

Mr. RICHMOND. Thank you, Mr. Secretary.

We are in a process of fixing these massive flood insurance premium increases around the country and we are getting some pushback from FEMA in terms of what they can and can't do and I just wanted to get you—to ask you to commit to ensuring that FEMA implement all aspects of the legislation as soon as possible, as soon as it is signed into law by the President, passed by both chambers.

So can you commit to doing that?

Secretary JOHNSON. Yes sir.

Mr. RICHMOND. Second, I would move to TSA's use of small businesses. Usually it is difficult because small businesses didn't have the money and expertise to invest in the specific technologies, but they are there, and TSA has failed to use them. In fact, they just awarded a $68 million contract to a company just as a small business is about to be certified and able to do that.

So can you commit to us to ensuring that you put pressure on TSA to use small businesses?

Secretary JOHNSON. I would encourage all of my components to look at the most effective and efficient way to contract out services.

My general view is that big is not necessarily better. I would rather have somebody who is more effective, was cost-efficient, is, you know, a little hungry and is looking to fulfill my mission in a cost-effective, efficient way.

Big is not necessarily better.

Mr. RICHMOND. I would just ask you to look in that specific instance of the business that is nearing certification. The fact that I think we may have contracted out all of the opportunity for them without taking into account the fact that they could be included.

The other thing I would follow up with or conclude with is Coast Guard reauthorization and the fact that I will publicly state on the record that, in the aftermath of both Katrina and Rita, watching the Coast Guard and what they do and how they did it, they are certainly a key component to homeland security. I would just urge that we stake our claim to jurisdiction and make sure that, that legislation—reauthorization would come before us and have your commitment to support us on that.

Secretary JOHNSON. I am very focused on Coast Guard re-capitalization at the moment. I am told that the Coast Guard is the most aged fleet of vessels in the world—I don't know whether that is true or not, but that is what I am told—and I think it is time for re-capitalization.

It is something I am focused on. I appreciate the support we have been given from Congress thus far.

Mr. RICHMOND. Thank you, and I will yield back the balance——

Chairman MCCAUL. On that note, let me just say we—I intend to offer a Coast Guard reauthorization bill.

With that, last but not least, the gentleman from Mississippi, Mr. Palazzo.

Mr. PALAZZO. Thank you, Mr. Chairman. Thank you, Secretary Johnson for being here today.

Mr. Secretary, I want to highlight an issue that is intimately related to FEMA, Hurricane Katrina, Hurricane Sandy, and other storms that may have flown under your radar so far since your confirmation.

I am talking about flood insurance, this rising cost and the multiple shortcomings of FEMA to get their flood mapping or premium rate setting right. There are countless instances where FEMA has used inaccurate or outdated data concerning land elevation and landscape features, and in some cases data that is decades old.

Much of this is detailed in the 2008 GAO report.

The House has been working on H.R. 3370, the Homeowner Flood Insurance Affordability Act. This bill will provide relief to homeowners who went to great efforts and expense and followed all the rules to build back after storms such as Hurricane Katrina and Sandy.

This bill will prevent FEMA from changing the rules and punishing those people when FEMA updates their flood maps. I urge my colleagues to support H.R. 3370 when it hits the floor, hopefully next week.

Now, while H.R. 3370 will go a long way to providing relief, we still need to ensure that FEMA is using good science and rating methods.

So Mr. Secretary, I know you are relatively new to your post, but this is a critical priority that needs to be addressed. Because FEMA and the NIFP fall under your purview as the head of DHS, I am curious, have you been made aware of the flawed and outdated formula FEMA has been using for premium rate setting? Are you aware of the way FEMA's faulty mapping practices and data are directing affecting the severity of rate increases for homeowners?

Secretary JOHNSON. Well, first of all, I think the overall goal for us in the Executive and Congressional branches is that we maintain going forward a solvent flood insurance program for the American people. That is the overarching priority.

I am aware of discussions, disagreements concerning maps. I was in one as recently as 2 days ago with a certain Governor who had raised concerns about the maps. I do know that when we adopt maps there is an opportunity for public community comment on the maps, and an appeal process so that local communities can raise concerns with the technique that we have used, that, that process is built into the law and I would encourage local communities that have concerns to raise those in the process.

Mr. PALAZZO. Well, Mr. Secretary, I appreciate that, and you know, the bill that is going forward in the House right now, it is a Nation-wide bipartisan issue. It is affecting homeowners. It is affecting communities. It is deteriorating property values. Just in my district alone, we are already seeing foreclosures because rates have gone from $1,000 to $11,000.

We could get into the unintended consequences of bigger waters, but this bill that we are gonna be introducing is paid for, it helps lead NFIP to become solvent, but it does it in a compassionate manner by not punishing those who have already played by the rules that FEMA and the local governments have set.

So, I look forward to working with you on that.

I yield back.

Chairman MCCAUL. Mr. Secretary, let me just say, thank you for your generosity with time.

I look forward to working with you on our priorities that I know we share together.

Members may have additional questions in writing. We ask that you respond to those.

Without objection, the committee now stands adjourned.

[Whereupon, at 12:24 p.m., the committee was adjourned.]

APPENDIX

QUESTION FROM CHAIRMAN MICHAEL T. MCCAUL FOR HONORABLE JEH C. JOHNSON

Question. The Congressional EMP Commission and numerous other experts have expressed concern about the vulnerability of the Nation's critical infrastructure to damage from a catastrophic EMP event as a result of a high-altitude EMP attack against the United States or a solar geomagnetic storm. These studies also warn that the Nation's current lack of EMP preparedness should be a top priority for National and homeland security. Please describe DHS activities related to the EMP threat and its potential impacts and consequences to the Nation's critical infrastructures.

Answer. The Department of Homeland Security (DHS) is working collaboratively, both internally and with external stakeholders, to reduce the risk from Electromagnetic Pulse and solar weather. Within the National Protection and Programs Directorate (NPPD), the Office of Cyber and Infrastructure Analysis[1]—and the Office of Cybersecurity and Communications have worked to model and assess Electromagnetic Pulse effects, and to conduct research and propose solutions to understand and mitigate Electromagnetic Pulse risks. For example, NPPD conducted a study in 2010 on Electromagnetic Pulse's potential impact on extra-high voltage transformers and recommended options for hardening these systems from Electromagnetic Pulse attacks.

Further, the Science and Technology Directorate's (S&T) Recovery Transformer (RecX) project is intended to increase the resilience of the power grid. A pilot demonstration was successfully conducted in March 2012 in which an extra-high voltage transformer prototype was transported, installed, and energized in less than 1 week. DHS S&T and RecX project partners are working on transition plans for RecX with various stakeholders, including Federal partners and private industry. Additionally, the Resilient Electric Grid program under DHS S&T increases the resilience of the grid, particularly in urban areas, by enabling substations to interconnect with one another in order to share power and assets in the event of an emergency, via an inherently fault-current-limiting high-temperature super-conducting cable. The Resilient Electric Grid program will demonstrate this new capability in a pilot installation with our partner utility, Consolidated Edison, later this year. S&T has also developed modeling and simulation capabilities that are capable of analyzing the impact of blasts, Electromagnetic Pulses, and other hazards on critical infrastructure. S&T has a fiscal year 2014 new start program, Solar Storm Mitigation, that will provide the capability to forecast geomagnetically-induced currents levels at specific nodes within the grid. This capability would allow the utility to take proactive operational measures to protect a given transformer from damage due to the impacts of a solar storm.

Other DHS components also have roles in building resilience. The Federal Emergency Management Agency (FEMA) has exercised scenarios involving Electromagnetic Pulse and solar weather and is developing plans to help address these evolving threats. FEMA is also working with States and industry to reduce the risk from Electromagnetic Pulse, notably by deploying new capabilities as part of the integrated public alert and warning system to help keep the public informed and alerted during a major Electromagnetic Pulse event. Additionally, DHS coordinates Unclassified and Classified briefings and workshops for industry and works to analyze their vulnerabilities and demonstrate potential impacts and costs if those vulnerabilities are left unaddressed.

---

[1] In February 2014, NPPD created the Office of Cyber and Infrastructure Analysis by integrating analytic resources from across NPPD including the Homeland Infrastructure Threat and Risk Analysis Center and the National Infrastructure Simulation and Analysis Center which were formerly located within the NPPD Office of Infrastructure Protection.

QUESTIONS FROM HONORABLE PATRICK MEEHAN FOR HONORABLE JEH C. JOHNSON

Question 1. We are concerned about the EAGLE II procurement and the Department's corrective action to re-evaluate bids. As you know, Members of this committee, have been watching how the Department has handled—really mishandled, this massive contract procurement. What we have witnessed has not given us comfort in the Department's administrative capabilities. The procurement took almost 3 years between the time proposals were submitted and contract awards were finally completed last fall. Since that time, the Department has been besieged by protests—I believe there are over 40 protests pending. Clearly, there are many groups that feel this procurement was flawed. At the end of December, we were informed that the Department was taking corrective action to re-evaluate bids, but have not had received an update since. Could you comment on the status of the Department's correction action and a time line for when this process will be concluded?

Answer. The Enterprise Acquisition Gateway for Leading Edge Solutions II procurement consisted of 9 distinct competitions across 3 functional requirements categories. The Department of Homeland Security began awarding contracts 21 months after proposals were received and completed contract awards within 31 months.

Contract awards have been made in all nine Enterprise Acquisition Gateway for Leading Edge Solutions II award tracks in an open and transparent process employing Federal procurement best practices and in accordance with the Federal Acquisition Regulation. Out of the 9 competitions, 6 are available for immediate use, while 3 are in the final stages of the procurement process. To date, awards have been made to large and small companies—task order awards have been made to companies in all three functional categories.

The Department of Homeland Security recognizes that protests are part of the procurement process in accordance with the Federal Acquisition Regulation. For Enterprise Acquisition Gateway for Leading Edge Solutions II, a significant number of protests have been received, many of which have been dismissed or withdrawn. However, protests add significant time to the overall procurement cycle.

In addition to agency level and Government Accountability Office protests, interested parties may also protest the acquisition through the United States Court of Federal Claims.

Based upon the significant number of offerors protesting the award decisions, the Department of Homeland Security decided that re-evaluation of proposals in some functional categories and tracks is the most effective and efficient way of addressing the concerns raised, while ensuring fairness in this competitive process. This will allow the most expeditious path to completion. The Department has completed all re-evaluations.

Question 2. I remain concerned about the impact delays will have on the Department's ability to provide mission-critical services to secure our Nation's borders. Given the problems with the Eagle II procurement, is the Department providing the flexibility (exceptions or waivers) to component agencies that generally use this vehicle, so they have the ability to move their work elsewhere to ensure they are able to provide mission-critical services?

Answer. As of March 26, 2014, four of the awarded Enterprise Acquisition Gateway Leading Edge Solutions II tracks are fully available for use. Department of Homeland Security contracting offices have the flexibility to satisfy current mission requirements through an "exception" to the use of Enterprise Acquisition Gateway for Leading Edge Solutions II without the Office of the Chief Procurement Officer's approval. In addition to 6 specified exceptions, contracting officers may request a waiver from the Office of the Chief Procurement Officer to purchase goods or services from an alternative contract source. The Office of the Chief Procurement Officer has received a total of 25 waiver requests and all but one of these requests was approved.

QUESTIONS FROM HONORABLE TOM MARINO FOR HONORABLE JEH C. JOHNSON

Question 1. Immigration and Customs Enforcement, known as ICE, and the National Intellectual Property Rights Coordination Center, known as the IPR Center, both play vital roles in the battle against theft of our Nation's intellectual property. In your new capacity, I strongly encourage you to ensure adequate resources within the Department are provided to assist in their missions to protect our citizens from dangerous products, and to guard against the criminals and terrorists who traffic in illicit, illegal, and counterfeit goods. Research has shown that IP theft is truly a matter of National security—such as counterfeit memory chips found in our military aircrafts in 2010. In your new role, can we count on you to provide the various agencies within the Department with the funding and resources they need to effectively fight IP theft?

Question 2. Further, do you have any ideas on how we can better strengthen these programs to protect against future threats?

Answer. Yes, I will continue to work with Congress to ensure the Department of Homeland Security (DHS) continues to provide the funding and resources necessary to ensure that it remains the leading U.S. Government agency for combating intellectual property crimes. Enforcing intellectual property laws remains a priority for both DHS's U.S. Immigration and Customs Enforcement (ICE) and U.S. Customs and Border Protection (CBP). The ICE-led National Intellectual Property Rights Coordination Center (IPR Center) is a collaborative effort supported by 17 U.S. Government agencies, Interpol, Europol, and the governments of Canada and Mexico to enhance enforcement of intellectual property and trade fraud violations that threaten the U.S. economy, endanger public health and safety, and threaten America's military personnel. The IPR Center integrates law enforcement efforts with private industry information in the exchange of tactical intelligence and joint operations.

ICE, CBP, the IPR Center, and partner agencies have developed initiatives to address some of the most pressing threats from intellectual property infringement. Operation Chain Reaction combats counterfeit and substandard parts within the U.S. Department of Defense and U.S. Government supply chains. Operation Engine Newity targets the importation and distribution of counterfeit and substandard automotive products that pose a health and safety risk. Pursuant to this operation, investigations conducted by ICE Homeland Security Investigations (HSI) and the Federal Bureau of Investigation, as well as interdictions made by CBP, have uncovered counterfeit airbags, steering, braking, and seat belt components. Operation Apothecary addresses, analyzes, and attacks potential vulnerabilities in the customs entry process that allow for the smuggling of commercial quantities of counterfeit, unapproved, and/or adulterated drugs. Operation In Our Sites identifies, targets, and seizes internet domain names that defraud U.S. consumers and businesses by trafficking infringing goods, pursuing assets, and criminally prosecuting principals. Recognizing the importance of protecting our own supply chain from counterfeit goods, ICE has developed counterfeit awareness, mitigation, identification, and reporting training for ICE purchase card holders and approvers via ICE acquisition office-hosted webinars. Additionally, the IPR Center coordinates National and international operations that focus on the security of the supply chain and protect the U.S. economy and American jobs. Congressional support, such as appropriation for these initiatives and assistance in raising constituent awareness about the dangers of counterfeit products can assist DHS in effectively fighting intellectual property theft.

QUESTIONS FROM HONORABLE MARK SANFORD FOR HONORABLE JEH C. JOHNSON

Question 1a. Is individual privacy a priority for the Department of Homeland Security?

Answer. Protecting privacy is critical within the DHS mission. The Homeland Security Act of 2002 established the Privacy Office within DHS. The Homeland Security Act established the DHS chief privacy officer as the first statutorily-created privacy officer in the Federal Government. The chief privacy officer reports directly to the Secretary and is charged with "assuring that the use of technologies sustains, and do not erode, privacy protections relating to the use, collection and disclosure of personal information." Pursuant to this mandate, the Privacy Office works to ensure that the protection of privacy rights is incorporated into the Department's programs, policies, and procedures.

The Privacy Office's division into four major functional areas—Compliance, Policy, Oversight, and Disclosure—has positioned it to ensure involvement with programs, offices, and initiatives across the Department at each stage of the development life cycle—from planning and design, through implementation and, possibly, retirement. The Privacy Office calls this process "operationalizing" privacy.

The foundation of this process begins with privacy compliance. The Privacy Office's Compliance team manages this by ensuring that the agency has published in the *Federal Register* a System of Records Notice for all Privacy Act systems of records. In addition, the Compliance team ensures that all personally identifiable information contained in these Privacy Act Systems of Records as well as within any electronic record systems is handled in full compliance with fair information practice principles, as set forth in the Privacy Act of 1974 and E-Government Act. The Compliance team also works closely with Component Privacy Officers, who are embedded in programs and offices across the Department. This collaboration has facilitated the Privacy Office's understanding and reach into projects at the earliest stages of program and system planning, including those related to transportation-, border-, and cybersecurity. These efforts are reflected in the hundreds of Privacy Impact Assessments published on the DHS Privacy Office public-facing website: *www.dhs.gov/privacy*. These Privacy Impact Assessments support transparency, and give the public a detailed look into DHS efforts to secure the border, protect the transportation system, ensure that critical infrastructure is protected from cyber threats, and the whole range of DHS missions that may include collecting personal information. These Privacy Impact Assessments also analyze potential privacy risks and detail the steps the Department takes to mitigate those risks.

The Privacy Policy team assesses novel privacy challenges that are raised during the privacy compliance process, either through the use of new technologies or methods of fulfilling our Department's vast mission set. Examples include the Policy team's engagement on the Department's information sharing in support of "big data" counterterrorism programs, and its support for DHS's international activities, which must account for other countries' differing requirements and expectation about privacy.

The Oversight team in the Privacy Office ensures that programs are effectively mitigating potential privacy risks discussed in compliance documentation—like Privacy Impact Assessments—and helps to identify and mitigate new risks that are discovered over time. Their pioneering use of Privacy Compliance Reviews has become an important tool for fine-tuning privacy protections in the Department's operational programs. The Oversight team is already designing a Privacy Compliance Review for many of DHS's cybersecurity activities.

Finally, the Privacy Office's Disclosure team is responsible for providing individuals and the public with appropriate access to and transparency for DHS records, following a request for access either under the Privacy Act or the Freedom of Information Act. The Disclosure team pursues proactive, timely disclosure of information about DHS programs, operations, systems, and policies in a manner that is easily accessible to the public. Additionally, the Disclosure team provides policy and compliance leadership for Freedom of Information Act Officers across the Department.

Question 1b. What specific steps will you take to ensure the civil liberties of American citizens as they interact with DHS at our airports, along our borders, or at their home computers?

Answer. Given the volume of daily interactions DHS has with the public it is critical for us to diligently protect the civil rights and civil liberties of all persons. The Homeland Security Act established the Office for Civil Rights and Civil Liberties (CRCL) in section 705.

The Office for Civil Rights and Civil Liberties provides policy advice and internal oversight to ensure that civil rights and civil liberties are respected and not diminished. Many DHS components also have offices dedicated to civil rights and/or civil liberties policy and oversight. A major focus of CRCL's work is the initiation of investigations based on complaints received from the general public and non-Governmental organizations through U.S. mail, email, and fax, and the CRCL telephone hotline, as well as through the DHS Traveler Redress Inquiry Program. Incidents that merit investigation are also forwarded to CRCL from other offices at DHS and other Government agencies. Whether through recommendations arising from investigations, or its role in providing proactive advice to the Secretary and component leadership, CRCL is engaged in policy development throughout the Department.

CRCL supports the Transportation Security Administration (TSA) as it provides the highest level of security to all who pass screening checkpoints in a manner that also respects individual rights. For example, CRCL has worked with TSA on revised anti-profiling training for TSA's behavioral detection officers. Similarly, CRCL works with U.S. Customs and Border Protection on civil rights and civil liberties issues that can arise in border screening.

CRCL has also developed and implemented training for law enforcement officers and other DHS personnel who interact with travelers at the border to ensure that the civil rights and civil liberties of travelers are appropriately protected during the process of border screening.

In 2009, President Obama recognized the need to increase education and dialogue about cybersecurity. The President directed a Cyberspace Policy Review, which resulted in recommendations that have become the blueprint from which our Nation's cybersecurity foundation will grow to support an assured and resilient digital infrastructure. CRCL has been an integral part of the implementation of the recommendations stemming from that review, advising DHS cybersecurity professionals, managers, and leaders on how to protect individual rights while improving the Nation's cybersecurity posture across a range of cybersecurity initiatives conducted by the Department.

DHS efforts have focused on securing the Federal Government's networks—the ".gov" domain—while providing assistance to help secure critical infrastructure and the Nation's private cyber infrastructure using means other than Government monitoring of internet communications. The Department provides threat information, technical assistance, and coordination of National-level preparedness and response efforts for critical infrastructure owners and operators, State, local, and Tribal governments, foreign partners, and the general public, to assist them as they work with us to improve cybersecurity.

CRCL and the DHS Privacy Office also took an active role in implementing Executive Order 13636, which focuses Federal cybersecurity efforts securing the Nation's critical infrastructure. The Executive Order directed the annual completion of Privacy and Civil Liberties Assessments of activities conducted under the Executive Order, and the compilation of assessment reports from other Departments and agencies involved implementation activities. Working in close partnership with the DHS Privacy Office, CRCL completed assessments of Executive Order-related cybersecurity activities conducted by DHS, to ensure those activities appropriately address any privacy and civil liberties issues associated with those activities.

At the same time, CRCL and the DHS Privacy Office worked to ensure the interagency task force operated in a transparent manner, co-hosting meetings with advocacy groups and others focused on cybersecurity, privacy, and civil liberties issues. Concurrently, CRCL and the Privacy Office co-chaired the Privacy and Civil Liberties Assessments working group, 1 of 9 working groups established by the DHS-led Interagency Task Force charged with carrying out the directives of the Executive Order, and Presidential Policy Directive (PPD) 21, which advances a National unity of effort to strengthen and maintain secure, functioning, and resilient critical infrastructure. Together, CRCL and the Privacy Office shared best practices with privacy and civil liberties office colleagues from the participating Departments and agencies, and worked through the Assessments Working Group to manage the assessment reporting process.

Question 2. The Transportation Subcommittee heard testimony on November 14, 2013 from Administrator Pistole and others on TSA's Behavior Detection & Analysis Program (BDA) and its Behavior Detection Officers. Do you support the continuation of this program in light of GAO's report that there is no proof that it works after nearly $1 billion has been spent on it in the last 5 years without identifying a single terrorist?

Answer. Behavior detection techniques have been an accepted practice for many years within law enforcement, customs and border enforcement, Department of Defense, and security communities, both in the United States and internationally. The Transportation Security Administration's (TSA) Screening of Passengers by Observation Techniques (SPOT) behavior detection program is an important element of the TSA multi-layered security approach. TSA's Behavior Detection Officers (BDO) also play a key role in carrying out TSA's risk-based screening (RBS) initiatives. RBS initiatives are intended to provide a more common-sense, less-invasive screening experience for low-risk passengers.

Because TSA's overall security posture is composed of interrelated parts, to disrupt one piece of the multi-layered approach will have a far-reaching adverse impact on other pieces, thereby negatively affecting TSA's overall mission performance.

Additionally, in April 2011, the Department of Homeland Security Science and Technology Directorate completed a comprehensive study that examined the validity of using behavior indicators. The study found that the SPOT program provided a number of screening benefits and is more effective than random selection at identifying high-risk passengers.

Since the publication of the 2011 Study, TSA has taken steps to improve the entirety of the behavior detection program and the process by which it is validated. In early 2012, TSA began another round of research aimed at further substantiating the behavioral indicators and improving the detection protocols. This effort evolved into what is now known as the Behavior Detection Optimization effort. Optimization encompasses four pillars of behavior detection: (1) Improving recruiting processes, (2) Enhancing training content to further enhance BDO skill sets, (3) Instituting greater management and quality control systems, and (4) Revising its Behavioral Indicator Reference Guide (BIRG) and designing a new referral methodology.

Concurrently and integral to the Optimization project is a comprehensive Operational Test designed to collect the data to validate behavior detection over and above what was seen during the original 2011 SPOT Validation Study. Scenario-driven testing will be used in addition to the outcome-based protocols used in the prior Study. Each of the GAO limitations discussed in their report will be mitigated to the maximum extent possible given the constraints of testing within an operational environment. Initial testing will begin in Fall 2014, and full data collection is planned for late Winter 2015.

Question 3. The Transportation Subcommittee also heard testimony on January 28, 2014, from Mr. Roderick Allison, assistant administrator for TSA's Office of Inspection on a GAO report regarding whether or not TSA's criminal investigators in the Office of Inspection met the criteria for Law Enforcement Availability Pay (LEAP). Have you reviewed this issue and are you in favor of changes to the status of these criminal investigators?

Answer. The Transportation Security Administration (TSA) is authorized under the Aviation and Transportation Security Act, Pub. L. 107–71 (ATSA), to establish and classify positions and compensate its workforce. TSA's criminal investigators receive Law Enforcement Availability Pay (LEAP) for unscheduled overtime pursuant to TSA policy, TSA Management Directive (MD) 1100.55–8, *Premium Pay,* and MD1100.88–1, *Law Enforcement Position Standards and Hiring Requirements.* TSA policy provides that for the purposes of law enforcement premium pay administration, the agency follows the provisions of 5 U.S.C. § 5545a, and 5 C.F.R. § 550.181 through § 550.186.

TSA's 1811 criminal investigators conduct criminal investigations of TSA employees and contractors, integrity testing, and external investigations. In accordance with both TSA policy and the referenced statute and regulatory provisions, TSA's 1811 criminal investigators must work, or be available to work, a minimum annual average of 2 hours of unscheduled overtime per non-excludable regular workday.

Pursuant to the Department of Homeland Security, Inspector General recommendation (from its September 2013 report entitled *Transportation Security Administration Office of Inspection's Efforts to Enhance Transportation Security,* not from a GAO report), TSA has an on-going effort to determine the appropriate number of criminal investigators within TSA. Following the completion of the review, TSA will determine the scope of any changes that should be made to staffing allocations and position classification within the Office of Inspection (OOI).

QUESTIONS FROM HONORABLE WILLIAM R. KEATING FOR HONORABLE JEH C. JOHNSON

Question 1a. Mr. Secretary, I have a question on a topic that I have been involved with since my days as a district attorney outside of Boston, Massachusetts, when a 16-year old named Delvonte Tisdale perished after he breached airport security and stowed away on a plane from Charlotte-Douglas to Boston Logan Airport. Since joining this committee in 2011, I have sat through several hearings on perimeter security and have heard numerous testimonies on the discouraging 2009 Government Accountability Office (GAO) report of Transportation Security Administration's (TSA) assessments. Following GAO recommendations, TSA published an assessment in July 2010—the Transportation Sector Security Risk Assessment (TSSRA)—that included various risk-based scenarios related to airport perimeter security but did not consider potential vulnerabilities of airports to an insider attack.

It is now 2014 and I remain unconvinced that TSA is capable of adequately securing ports of entry, and, earlier this month, I sent a letter to GAO Comptroller General Gene Dodaro requesting that GAO conduct a comprehensive review of the efficacy of the Transportation Security Administration's perimeter security assessments.

Can you elaborate on the Department's vision for ensuring perimeter security moving forward?

Answer. Commercial airports in the United States are required to establish and carry out measures for controlling entry, and to provide for detection of and response to unauthorized presence or movement in the controlled area. These plans are approved by the Transportation Security Administration (TSA),

Airport authorities, in partnership with State, and local law enforcement (including airport police and public safety departments), and overseen by TSA, enacts a layered and multi-faceted approach to increase perimeter security through regulation and inspection activities.

- First, TSA establishes regulatory requirements, such as Airport Security Programs (ASP) that must be adopted by regulated commercial airports, and inspects to those standards. TSA issues ASP changes and Security Directives to counter emerging threats or tactics that threaten airport perimeter security. TSA's Transportation Security Inspectors (TSI), perform inspections at regulated commercial airports. Perimeter security, including pedestrian access points, vehicle gates, and building access points, are a focus area of these inspections.
- Second, TSA maintains regular communication and partnering efforts with airport associations, including the American Association of Airport Executives (AAAE) and the Airports Council International—North America (ACI–NA), to promote increased vigilance and security.

- Third, TSA conducts numerous outreach efforts at the local level directly, including TSI Perimeter Security Outreaches and Joint Vulnerability Assessments (JVAs) and partnered with Federal, State, and local law enforcement to identify security weaknesses at airports including the perimeters.

Together, these efforts demonstrate TSA's vision of continuously improving airport perimeter security through risk-based efforts and partnership with affected stakeholders.

Question 1b. How effective has TSA's implementation of GAO's recommendations been?

Answer. In response to GAO 09–399, Transportation Security Administration (TSA) conducted a series of Special Emphasis Assessments (SEA) of airport perimeter security at all Category X through Category III airports in 2012. Local Transportation Security Inspectors (TSIs) gathered physical security data from the 284 affected airports. The data gathered from this SEA drove TSA's additional outreach efforts. Based on the identification of best practices and potential weaknesses, in 2013, TSIs worked with commercial airports to help them continue to identify areas for improvement and take action to increase perimeter security. All GAO questions related to regulatory compliance have been closed.

Using the results of the perimeter assessments, outreach, and additional assessments, in 2013, TSA completed a Perimeter Security Risk Assessment which identified best practices and potential sources of risk in perimeter security. TSA posted the results to its web board, to which airport operators have access, and provided these results to GAO. TSA provided in-depth results to its Federal Security Directors in the field to discuss with their respective airports, allowing each airport operator to understand the airport's current state and where to address mitigation efforts. Airport operators responded favorably to TSA's assessment, outreach, and information-sharing efforts.

Question 1c. How do you plan on reallocating resources to ensure that necessary recommendations are enforced and our perimeters are adequately secured?

Answer. The Transportation Security Administration (TSA) has appropriate staffing and resources to accomplish its compliance mission. Over and above its continuous regulatory compliance inspections of perimeter security, in fiscal year 2014, TSA implemented targeted testing of security measures as a component of TSA's Compliance Security Enhancement Through Testing (COMSETT) protocols. TSA is using COMSETT to direct its limited Transportation Security Inspector force toward targeted critical aviation security tests in order to buy down risk. TSA will continue to use COMSETT in fiscal year 2015 and future years to identify the vulnerabilities that persist in perimeter security and will work with those particular airports to improve their access control security.

Question 2a. I believe there is no greater depiction of the state of current information sharing between intelligence agencies and our international partners than the events surrounding the Boston Marathon bombings last April. The Boston Police Commissioner, Ed Davis, sat before this committee last year to explain that information was held from him by the FBI that could have potentially served as a force multiplier in the search for the suspects following the attacks in Boston. Further, this committee ran into additional hurdles when we asked the FBI to testify before us both in public and secure settings. Instead of complying and walking us through what happened on that fateful day, the FBI cited bureaucratic, jurisdictional guidelines to explain why they did not need to share information with our committee (despite the fact that they have testified before the Homeland Security Committee in the past).

In response to further inquiries to both DHS and the FBI, Chairman McCaul and I were able to find some discrepancies in communication between those two agencies, as well. In the lead up to the Boston bombings, Tamerlan Tsarnaev's questionable past and travels in and out of Dagestan, did cause enough alarm to even designate him for a second screening. FBI and DHS are supposed to work together when individuals are flagged in the databases.

In this regard, Mr. Secretary, what can we do to make sure that there is not only adequate information sharing across the agencies, but also between Federal and local entities during a mass casualty event?

Question 2b. What is the biggest hindrance to better coordination?

Question 2c. Nearly 13 years after 9/11, I am still concerned that, despite the improvements, there are still serious gaps that need to be addressed.

Answer. On a daily basis, DHS and the Federal Bureau of Investigation, along with other Federal agencies at all levels, coordinate and share information and intelligence regarding real and potential threats to our Nation. We do this through a number of mechanisms in offices and areas all across the Nation. DHS also works closely with our State and local partners to share investigative information, intelligence, and other Homeland Security information. DHS components routinely work along-side State and local partners on investigations and law enforcement operations, sharing the information necessary to protect our communities. In addition, we have placed DHS personnel in State and major urban area fusion centers for the express purpose of sharing intelligence and information with those best-postured in the States to share relevant information more broadly at the local level.

DHS recently completed its internal After-Action Review. We found that in the wake of the bombings, a large information void existed. Since the Boston attack, DHS, the FBI, and National Counterterrorism Center (NCTC) have expanded our ability to share information with State and local officials about potential threats. Examples of recent events where information has been shared include the 9/11 anniversary and the homeland security implications of the conflict in Syria. DHS identified ways to more effectively work with interagency partners at FBI Joint Terrorism Task Forces and sent updated guidance to officers in the field to improve such collaboration. DHS also continues to work closely with Federal partners to screen and vet domestic and international travelers, visa applicants, and other persons of interest to identify potential threats. After the Boston attack, DHS reviewed its name-matching capabilities, leading to improvements in its ability to detect variations of names derived from a wide range of languages.

In recent weeks DHS also completed an interagency review along with Department of Justice and Central Intelligence Agency of information handling and sharing prior to the bombing. This report, along with the DHS After-Action Report, are driving procedural and operational changes to the way DHS coordinates and collaborates with other Federal agencies, and how we share information with our State and local partners.

DHS is committed to continuing to share the most germane and meaningful data in its possession with other Federal agencies, and with our State and local trusted partners. Following the attack in Boston, DHS upgraded its name-matching capabilities, and issued guidance to its officers at the JTTFs to formalize communication practices to ensure practices regarding travel alerts are documented. DHS is also committed to continuing its work with the FBI to ensure effective information sharing. Boston is a reminder that we must continually strive to work together across Federal agencies to identify and share threat information with each other and among our State and local partners who ultimately will bear the brunt of any successful terrorist attack.

Question 3a. In the aftermath of the bombings, emergency response was key. I have spoken to several first responders, medical personnel, and law enforcement officials who said that the fact that so few people perished in Boston on April 16 was simply a miracle.

Are there efforts underway to make sure that all emergency responders carry a tourniquet as well as quick clot gauze to control traumatic bleeding?

Question 3b. Are there such efforts under way?

Answer. The Federal Emergency Management Agency (FEMA) in coordination with the DHS Office of Health Affairs (OHA) supports whole community preparedness for mass casualty incidents through a number of efforts, to include workshops and training, policy and doctrine, and grant programs.

Workshops

In partnership with the National Counterterrorism Center and the Federal Bureau of Investigation, FEMA's Office of Counterterrorism and Security Preparedness developed the Joint Counterterrorism Awareness Workshops in 2011. The Joint Counterterrorism Awareness Workshops (JCTAWS) bring together law enforcement, fire service, emergency medical services and the private-sector stakeholders to conduct scenario-based reviews of local prevention and response plans and capabilities. The workshop is based on a scenario in which multiple, coordinated assaults occur over a 24-hour period, similar to the November 2008 terrorist attacks in Mumbai, India. Since its inception in 2011, 15 JCTAWS sessions have been delivered with over 2,500 participants.

The workshops are designed to bring together law enforcement, fire, emergency medical services, and the private-sector stakeholders that would respond to complex terror event. Response protocols range broadly throughout the United States. Workshops have included representation from the following disciplines/fields: Local, State, and Federal law enforcement; State and local fusion centers; local and regional fire and emergency medical services responders; hotel/convention security; large sporting/commercial venues; private/public university; telecommunications; private/public infrastructure; and airport administrators/security.

Workshops have been conducted in the following locations:

- Monterey, CA—November 2010—Kickoff conference at Naval Post Graduate School
- Philadelphia, PA—January 31, 2011
- Boston, MA—March 10, 2011
- Sacramento, CA—May 10, 2011
- Indianapolis, IN—June 28, 2011
- Honolulu, HI—September 29, 2011
- Houston, TX—November 16, 2011
- Bethpage, NY—January 2012—Kickoff conference
- Nashville, TN—March 15, 2012
- Denver, CO—June 12, 2012
- Charlotte, NC—June 27, 2012 (Briefing of Lessons Learned) (Democratic National Convention)
- Tampa, FL—July 10, 2012 (Briefing of Lessons Learned) (Republican National Convention)
- Los Angeles, CA—July 31–August 1, 2012
- Las Vegas, NV—October 9–10, 2012
- Atlanta, GA—February 26–27, 2013
- Seattle, WA—June 18–19, 2013
- Minneapolis, MN—August 27–28, 2013
- Washington, DC—December 3–4, 2013
- Miami, FL—February 11–12, 2014

Workshops currently scheduled for calendar year 2014 include Oklahoma City, OK on June 16–17, 2014 and Orlando, FL on September 9–10, 2014.

Beginning in 2012, the workshop added a second day to address medical issues (pre-hospital, hospital, post-care) associated with a complex attack, including Tactical Emergency Casualty Care. A set of best practice treatment guidelines for trauma care in a high-threat, pre-hospital environment, the Tactical Emergency Casualty Care guidelines are built upon medical lessons learned by United States and allied military forces, as well as civilian mass casualty experiences both in the United States and abroad. The lessons learned have been modified to address the specific needs of civilian populations and civilian out-of-hospital practice, and address the use of tourniquets by all levels of first responders as well as the appropriate hemostatic agents. Tactical Emergency Casualty Care guidelines consider the requirements of a civilian population to include: Pediatric, geriatric, and special needs patients; underlying medical conditions common in a civilian population; characteristics and limitations of civilian providers; and the varied types of threats that responders face.

The DHS Office of Health Affairs (OHA) held a stakeholder engagement meeting in February to facilitate a discussion between subject-matter experts in the first-responder community on improving survivability in improvised explosive device (IED) and active-shooter incidents. OHA partnered with the Department of Health and Human Services (HHS) Office of the Assistant Secretary of Preparedness and Response (ASPR), and the Department of Transportation National Highway Traffic Safety Administration (NHTSA) Office of Emergency Medical Services on the meeting.

More than 250 representatives from across the country, from State, local, and Federal organizations in the fire, emergency medical services (EMS), law enforcement, emergency management, and other professions heard presentations from subject-matter experts and participated in panel and group discussions on hemorrhage control, personal protective equipment, and interoperability when responding to IED and active-shooter incidents. The group also reviewed response strategies from the U.S. military, focusing on the military's protocols for tourniquet use, discussed how to apply lessons learned in the civilian first-responder environment, and best practices from recent incidents in the United States. OHA brought the first responder groups together so that unique solutions that work for each community can be discussed and adopted at the State and local level. Some of the solutions developed included: Improving access to and training on hemorrhage control materials; increased education on PP&E equipment and how it can be most effectively used by all responders; improving working relationships, regular joint training and exercises, between fire, EMS, and law enforcement personnel at the local level; and targeting grants to facilitate interoperability.

Training

In addition to the JCTAWS, FEMA's emergency responder training courses currently offered by the National Preparedness Directorate's Center for Domestic Preparedness (CDP) and the National Training and Education Division (NTED) provide instruction on the use of tourniquets and quick clot gauze to control traumatic bleeding.

In its health care curriculum and specialized mass casualty response training, the CDP highlights and promotes best practices to include the use of tourniquets and quick clot gauze to control traumatic bleeding when practicable. CDP monitors National events and, when appropriate, incorporates best practices regarding response actions, techniques, tactics, and protocols into applicable training curriculum. Curriculum updates are made once the relevant National organization or governing authority promulgates acceptance of best practices through the creation of competency standards and training objectives.

Selected NTED training partners include emerging trends in the use of tourniquets and quick clot gauze to control traumatic bleeding in their courses. Texas Engineering Extension Service's *Medical Preparedness for Bombing Incidents* course specifically addresses tourniquets and quick clot gauze to control traumatic bleeding; and the American College of Emergency Physicians' *First Responder on the Scene Training* and Texas State University's *Active Threat Integration Response* courses (both under development) include details on these emergency medical response techniques. All NTED training partners use either the Tactical Emergency Casualty Care standard or the Department of Defense equivalent United States Military's Tactical Combat Casualty Care standard.

Policy

The DHS Office of Health Affairs (OHA) is leading a cross-Departmental working group on the development of Federal guidance for first responders on the medical response to improvised explosive device (IED) and active-shooter incidents. The ultimate goal of the document is to improve survivability of victims from IED and/or active-shooter incidents. Based on best practices and lessons learned, the guidance document will provide evidence-based information on the medical response to both IEDs and active-shooter incidents, with recommendations for hemorrhage control and tourniquet use, personal protective equipment for first responders, and interoperability between law enforcement, EMS, and fire professionals responding to IED and active-shooter incidents. The guidance is still under development, but will be posted on-line and distributed to the first-responder community.

The DHS OHA also participated with the Departments of Health and Human Services, Transportation, Justice, and Defense, and non-Governmental organizations in the development and subsequent publishing of an evidence-based guideline to standardize hemorrhage control treatment. Previously, no consistent standard existed for local and State medical officials and responders.

Grant Programs

For years, FEMA's preparedness grant programs have provided funding in support of a wide range or prevention, protection, response, recovery, and mitigation activities. Funds may be used to support the purchase of critical medical supplies including medications and equipment, training, and exercises to prepare for and respond to mass casualty incidents. Within FEMA's recently released fiscal year 2014 preparedness grant program funding opportunity announcements, mass casualty incident preparedness and response was emphasized to stress the activities that build capabilities surrounding immediate emergency victim care. This includes:

- Improving emergency care to victims of mass casualty events, including mass shootings;
- Improving community first aid training;
- Enhancing the integration of local emergency management, public health, and health care systems into a coordinated, sustained, local capability to respond effectively to a mass casualty incident;
- Demonstrating how grantees' investments will increase the effectiveness of emergency preparedness planning and response for the whole community by integrating and coordinating activities for vulnerable populations including children, the elderly, pregnant women, and individuals with disabilities and others with access and functional needs;
- Encouraging collaboration with local, regional, and State public health and health care partners; and
- Encouraging engagement in preparedness efforts across first-responder community, including EMS for response to catastrophic events and acts of terrorism.

With support from FEMA's preparedness grant funds, Boston has purchased tourniquets for all first responders, and EMS units carry the quick clot gauze. We are aware of plans to have kits that include multiple tourniquets and quick clot gauze strategically positioned at special events for quick deployment in the event of an incident.

Question 4. In November, I requested an independent review of Massachusetts' new flood maps by two coastal scientists affiliated with the University of Massachusetts—Dartmouth's School of Marine Science and Technology and Applied Coastal Research and Engineering, specifically using the town of Marshfield as a test case. Their findings, detailed in a White Paper, indicated that FEMA used a mapping method tailored for the Pacific Coast instead of developing one correct for New England. As a result, FEMA likely over-predicted flooding that would occur during a 100-year storm for much of the State. The town of Rockport's recent successful appeal on the basis of demonstrating that there was more accurate scientific data available is further evidence that the new flood maps must be fixed. Homeowners have a right to know that FEMA is using the best available scientific technology when drawing the flood maps. I ask that FEMA work with us on a plan to fix the Commonwealth's flood maps utilizing the best available scientific data that is appropriate for our geographic region or suspend the new flood maps until a decision is made to amend them. Too much is at stake for our homeowners and communities to not get this right. Can you please elaborate on what methods FEMA is utilizing to certify to communities that these maps are drawn using the best available scientific models?

Answer. The goal of the coastal Flood Insurance Rate Map updates in Massachusetts is to provide our communities with credible flood hazard and risk information on which they can make sound mitigation and insurance decisions. Throughout the early stages of the coastal Flood Insurance Study, FEMA engaged community officials and State partner agencies to ensure the best available local data was used. Engaging local officials to incorporate locally-available data and using scientifically-credible methodologies helps to ensure that the flood hazard information portrayed on the Flood Insurance Rate Maps represents an accurate characterization of local flooding conditions.

Once the preliminary Flood Insurance Rate Map information is developed, FEMA releases this information for public review and holds a formal appeal period during which additional information may be submitted through the community to refine the preliminary flood maps. If an alternative methodology is available and meets certain standards, it can be accepted for use in the Flood Insurance Rate Maps. As you note, the town of Rockport recently submitted modeling that follows an alternative approach that meets appropriate technical standards. While this approach does not negate the results determined as part of the FEMA analysis, we reviewed it and were able to incorporate it into the on-going update for the town of Rockport.

The Rockport example is a model of successful coordination between FEMA and local communities because they submitted an alternative approach in a timely manner; FEMA is actively working through a similar process with the State and other Massachusetts communities.

○